Three White Dogs Cookbook

A Five-Ingredient or less Canine Cookbook Filled with Fun Facts

P.J. Blue

iUniverse, Inc.
New York   Bloomington

Three White Dogs Cookbook
A Five-Ingredient or less Canine Cookbook Filled with Fun Facts

iUniverse books may be ordered through booksellers or by contacting:

iUniverse
1663 Liberty Drive
Bloomington, IN 47403
www.iuniverse.com
1-800-Authors (1-800-288-4677)

ISBN: 978-1-4401-0058-1 (pbk)
ISBN: 978-1-4401-0287-5 (ebk)

Printed in the United States of America

DEDICATION

This book is dedicated to my loving Bichon Frisé, Bailey, who lived to be 22 years old and to my three happy, healthy and adorable Bichon Frisés who are on the cover: Casey, the mother, Scruffy, the father, and Sky, their little girl.

Also, to all the dogs that hopefully will be eating delicious meals their masters have prepared for them. They are so loving and devoted to us, so please consider cooking for them. They may even love you more, if that is possible, and you won't be alone in the kitchen!

For more information, visit:
www.threewhitedogs.com

ACKNOWLEDGEMENTS

I could not have written this book without my three adorable white dogs, Casey, Scruffy, and Sky. They are the reason I wrote this book; in the hope that everyone who reads these recipes will start cooking for their own dog.

The support of my daughter, Christi, her husband, Paul, and my two adorable grandchildren, Travis and Jordan, were crucial to me as I was writing this book. My grandsons kept asking, "Grandma, are you done with your book yet?" My daughter was feeding her dog the same dry dog food day after day, and now she is cooking recipes from the book. She loves every minute of it when she sees how happy her dog Cash is as he gobbles up her delights.

The support of my friends in Chandler, AZ has been paramount in my writing. My friend Pam Parkinson-Mackey, Stuart Preston, my business coach and advisor, and to my friends who live in Tucson, AZ, Dona, Joel and Shannon Strabala and Sandy Wahl, who were cheering me on from afar. Also, to the members of the Chandler Chamber of Commerce, thank you for your encouragement and support.

Last but not least, to my manuscript writer, Jacob Roberts and to Steve Adams, of Studio Creations Photography, for the wonderful cover pictures for the book.

A portion of the proceeds of this book will be gladly donated to the National Canine Cancer Foundation.

Table of Contents

INTRODUCTION . . . . **xi**

Dog Section I **1**

    WHY A HOMEMADE DIET? 3
    THE HISTORY OF DOG FOOD 3

Dog Section II **5**

    BAKING TIPS 7
    FOOD TIDBITS 15
    RECIPE TIDBITS 19
    DOG TREATS 21
    HEALTHY DOG TREATS 23
    BAKED DOG TREATS 24
    NO BAKE DOG TREATS 39
    DOG RECIPES 53

Dog Section III **87**

    FUN FACTS 89
    DOG NAMES 99
    PET TRUSTS 101
    PUPPY BEHAVIOR 102
    MOVIES FEATURING DOGS 103
    FAMOUS NOVELS FEATURING DOGS 105
    DOGS IN MYTHOLOGY 106
    DOGS THAT HAVE APPEARED IN COMMERCIALS . .108
    COMIC STRIPS THAT FEATURE DOGS 109
    SPACE DOGS 110
    PRESIDENTS AND THEIR DOGS 111
    PRESIDENTS AND THE BREEDS THEY OWNED 113
    OFFICIAL STATE DOGS 114

INTERESTING DOG TALES OF FAMOUS
CELEBRITIES. 115
FAMOUS PEOPLE AND THEIR DOGS 116
BULLDOGS THAT WERE USED AS MASCOTS. 122
GO DOGGIE GREEN. 123
ASTROLOGY SIGNS. 125
BIRTHSTONES 130
SOME COMMON DOG SAYINGS 132

Dog Section IV **135**

BREED BEHAVIOR. 137
BREED TIDBITS 139
SMALL AND LARGE BREEDS. 140
HOUND GROUP. 141
SPORTING GROUP 142
TERRIER GROUP 143
NON-SPORTING GROUP. 145
WORKING AND HERDING GROUP 146
MIXED BREEDS 148
AFFECTIONATE AND FRIENDLY. 150
DOMINANT AND PROTECTIVE 151
TRAINABLE AND CLEVER DOGS. 152
GOOD NATURED 153
HOME LOVING DOGS 154
INDEPENDENT AND PERSONABLE 155
DOG CARE. 156
DENTAL HEALTH 156
POISONOUS PLANTS 158
DOG SAFETY TIPS 159

Cat Section V **161**

CAT TREATS 164
CAT RECIPES. 169

INTRODUCTION

Do you *love* to cook?
Do you *hate* to cook?

Then this is the book for you!

Are you feeding your dog the same food over and over again, night after night and month after month?
He still eats the same food, night after night, month after month, because that is what his *best friend* feeds him! Unlike humans, he doesn't complain or moan so everything is fine, right? *Wrong!*
Canned or dried, expensive or less expensive, name brand or "off" brand, do you really know what is in the dog food you are buying? You probably don't. But *you will know* what is in the food you are giving your lovable dog when you cook for him. *You* will have control of every ingredient. You will not add any artificial coloring, preservatives, or food unfit for canine consumption.
By now you might be saying, "WHO ME?" I am overworked and too stressed out to cook for my dog. What do you think your dog's response might be? How about, "Excuse me, am I not a member of this family? Don't I deserve to have fresh and healthy meals?" Well, *of course they do*!
The purpose of writing this book is for your dog. It is for his health and eating pleasure. Let's be honest, your dog gives you devotion, affection and love, perhaps even more than a human has ever given you. Even if you mess up the recipe, he will still wag his tail and want seconds. The chances of you messing up are small though because all the recipes in this book contain five ingredients or less, using ingredients you have in your kitchen, and with instructions that are easy to follow.
This is not just another dog cookbook. It is a potpourri of fun and interesting facts and trivia that will help you have a greater appreciation for your four-legged friend. The last chapter of the book is for the mixed households that have both dogs and cats. There are cat treats and cat recipes that the feline of the family will love.
Your dog doesn't care what kind of house it lives in, what kind of car you drive, what your income is or what clothes you have in your closet. They are by your side and love you for you. Make their life as enjoyable as they make yours.

Dog Section I

WHY A HOMEMADE DIET?

We love our pets as our family members. One of the best things we can do for them is to feed them a homemade diet. The recipes in this book are easy to follow and very healthy, because YOU control all the ingredients. Your dog will not eat any artificial colorings, additives or chemical preservatives. They will receive an enormous amount of vitamins and minerals from the array of the different ingredients that they will be eating.

Your dog's evolution derived from their ancestors, the wolves and they did not eat out of a can or eat bagged food. When you cook for your dog, make it fun. Variety is the spice of life. You wouldn't want to eat the same food day after day, so why should your dog? After all, he is a loving family member. So, get in that kitchen and rattle those pots and pans.

THE HISTORY OF DOG FOOD

An Ohio electrician was the first to market processed dog "cakes" in 1860. While in London, he noticed that stray dogs were on the docks near the sea eating the food that the sailors threw off the ship. He returned home and after thinking about this, he devised a "cake" made of beef blood, vegetables, and wheat. He sold these "cakes" in tins with pictures of various dogs on them. Then around 1907, a manufacturer made dog "biscuits" and these were introduced as a "complete food."

These "cakes" and "biscuits" were all that was available until around the 1920s. Then automobiles replaced many of the horses that were used as a means of transportation. Horses then became the first meat used for canned dog food. But then World War I caused a shortage in tin, which was what the horse meat was packaged in. Through supply and demand, dry dog food was introduced around 1945 and packaged in paper bags.

Today, entire grocery aisles are devoted to dry dog foods, canned dog foods, dog treats, dog bones, dog biscuits and dog toys.

Processed Dog Food (What's In It)

The Pet Food Crisis of 2007 sent us all reeling. Dogs and cats were dying from exposure to the wheat gluten and rice protein that were contaminated with melamine (an industrial chemical) and cyanuric acid. When these two products were combined, they had a devastating impact in the pet food. Many pet food companies do not make their own food. They give their recipes to manufacturing companies to make their products. So if there is a contaminated product, it can get into other foods that are manufactured at the same facility.

There is new awareness in the pet loving community to the potential dangers that lurk in many processed pet food packages. The FDA is currently inspecting less than five percent of the imported shipments of our pet foods, so the risk of another pet food recall could be quite high. Also, the all-natural and organic companies may also be affected by contamination because they also could be utilizing the same overseas factories that manufacture the pet food. Commercial pet food consumers need to be vigilant in knowing the origins of the food they are feeding to their beloved pets.

Here are some common definitions that can be found on dog food labeling:

ANIMAL BYPRODUCT: Has rendered meat that contains fat and water and does not fit into other definitions.

MEAT BYPRODUCT: Contains clean animal parts other than the meat, and can include livers, blood, bones, stomachs, lungs, brains and spleens. These byproducts cannot, however, contain the hair, hooves or teeth of animals.

MEAT MEAL: This is processed byproduct to remove fat and water with the blood, hoof, stomach, horns, and hides. But it may also contain dead, diseased, disabled and dying animals, known as the "4D's."

MEAT AND BONE MEAL: It is like the meat meal but it also includes bones, along with the meat, as well as the "4D's."

MEAT: If it states meat on the label, it is the clean flesh from slaughtered sheep, rabbits, pigs, goats, or cattle. Although, if the label says chicken, it must be from only chickens and not from the other animals listed.

Dog Section II

BAKING TIPS

If you bake treats for your dog, here is some information on the different types of flours that are available. Some dogs, like people, are sensitive to gluten. Gluten is the protein that creates the elasticity in dough.

Some flours are gluten-free and some come in a variety of textures and flavors. You can buy these different flours at a health food store, as well as the many supermarkets that are carrying the different types of flours that are listed.

Flaxseed Flour: High in Omega-3 fatty acids.

Tapioca Flour: Non-grain.

Corn Meal: Has a nice texture and is gluten-free.

White Flour: The most common but less nutritious.

Whole Wheat Flour: Has gluten in it. Store it in the refrigerator after opening.

Soy Flour: Is the hulled soybean and is non-grain and high in fiber.

Oat Bran Flour: Has high fiber.

Oatmeal Flour: Has a nice texture.

Garbanzo Bean Flour: Made from chickpeas and is grain-free.

Barley Flour: Has gluten but is low in fat. Has high fiber but tends to be bland.

Rice Flour: Is gluten-free and makes dog biscuits light and crisp.

Buckwheat Flour: Is gluten-free.

TURKEY

Whole turkeys are very economical. Stock up during the holidays when they are on sale. Baking a turkey can make a week's worth of meals and dogs absolutely love turkey. The leftover turkey makes getting meals fast and convenient. Always remove the bag that contains the organs and cook them up separately. Rinse the turkey and pour a can of chicken broth over the turkey and sprinkle with garlic powder. This will also make a rich broth to use in your recipes. Bake according to the directions on the package. Turkey is a wonderful source of protein.

Turkey Tidbits:

🐾 Turkey legs, thighs and breasts are sold in separate packages. These separate pieces cook up faster   than roasting a whole turkey, which is more convenient in the summertime.

🐾 Fresh or frozen turkey burgers make a quick and easy meal. They can be fried very quickly in a little olive oil and cut into bite size pieces.

🐾 Turkey Kielbasa is pre-cooked and can be diced and used as a treat or in a meal.

🐾 Ground turkey is sold in one-pound packages. This cooks slower than ground beef, but makes delicious meals. The ground turkey may be fried in a little olive oil. There is no need to drain because there will be very little fat from the turkey.

🐾 The ground turkey "store brand" is used in the recipes. It is less expensive and has the same nutrients as the name brands.

🐾 Turkey bacon and sausage are also available.

CHICKEN

Chicken is widely used in the following recipes because it is so versatile. It can be baked, sautéed, boiled, poached, broiled, fried or roasted. A whole chicken can be put into a crock-pot to cook the whole day while you are at work. An oval crock-pot can hold two whole chickens at once. Remove the bag that contains the organs and cook separately. Rinse the chicken and place in the crock-pot. Do NOT add any liquid. As the chicken cooks slowly, it will create the richest chicken broth you have ever tasted. I add no seasonings to these chickens, as the natural flavor is outstanding. Remove the skin and all the bones from the chicken. Let the broth cool and refrigerate. The fat will congeal to the surface and you can remove the fat easily to use for chicken broth.

Besides cooking a whole chicken, the packages of legs, thighs and breasts also cook well in the crock-pot. These pieces are easier and faster to skin and de-bone than the whole chicken. The thighs only have one bone in them. The legs also have one bone in them but they also have a tiny sliver bone. Be sure you get this very thin bone out of the leg, as it could get caught in your dog's throat.

Chicken Chat:

🐾 Roasted deli chickens are very convenient for a quick meal.

🐾 Ground chicken comes in one pound packages and is very easy to use as there is no dicing or de-boning necessary.

🐾 Stock up on the frozen chicken tenders, thighs, breasts and legs when they are on sale.

🐾 Chicken livers, gizzards and hearts usually come packaged together and are used in the following recipes. Dogs truly love the organ meats and they are very nutritious.

FISH

Most dogs love fish. Canned salmon and tuna are excellent sources of protein. All sorts of fish can be used for recipes for your dog. You can use flounder, tilapia, sole, mackerel, trout, sardines, or catfish. Just be sure that all bones are removed before serving. You can substitute tuna or salmon for the protein portion in the recipes.

Fish Finds:

🐾 Canned, fresh or frozen salmon can be substituted in all the recipes. Fresh salmon is frequently on sale and very quick and easy to prepare. Buy the canned tuna that is packed in water versus those packed in oil to save on calories.

🐾 If using fresh salmon, be sure that all the bones are removed. However, the bones in canned salmon are very soft and digestible, so they don't have to be removed.

🐾 All sorts of fish can be used in recipes for your dog. You can use flounder, tilapia, sole, mackerel, trout, sardines or catfish. Just be sure that all bones are removed before serving.

🐾 Shellfish, such as shrimp or lobster, may also be used. These tend to be fairly pricey, so my recipes do not include them. You can certainly use shellfish for a substitution in the recipes if you like.

BEEF

The variety of beef is endless. The recipes in this book include ground beef, beef liver, stew meat, roasts, beef hot dogs and cubed steaks. Chuck roast steaks go on sale periodically and I stock up on those, as they are cook quickly. The beef roasts are so simple to prepare. In the summer, use your crock-pot to cook the roast all day. As a hint, I either put the crock-pot outside on the patio, or in the laundry room. It is amazing how much heat they give off into the room. In the winter, I always cook them in the oven to help heat the house up. Kitchen shears come in handy when cutting up the roasts.

Beef Blab:

Ground beef can be fried, baked, put in a crock-pot with some beef broth, or even boiled in beef broth and drained of the fat.

Beef liver is usually less expensive than chicken livers and is used in a variety of the recipes. The organ meats are a wonderful source of protein and nutrients. Limit them to no more than a few days a week, as they can cause loose stools. A good time to shop for livers is early in the morning or late at night when they usually go on sale.

Tenderized cubed steaks cook very quickly for a fast dinner.

Stew meat is another great ingredient because it also cooks very quickly and can be substituted in most of the beef recipes.

Most grocery stores have a dedicated discount section in the meat department. Watch for these specials and stock up.

STARCHES

Starches can consist of one third of your dog's total diet. It is best to use whole-wheat starches for their high fiber content. The starches used in the recipes include oatmeal, cornmeal, cornbread, pasta, white and brown rice, elbow macaroni, egg noodles and whole wheat bread.

🐾 Cook up a whole batch of rice, pasta or macaroni to have on hand for the whole week.

🐾 While your oven is on for something, stick in a potato or two to also have on hand for a recipe.

🐾 Whole-wheat pasta is preferred over white pasta for extra fiber and more nutrition.

🐾 Brown rice is a much better choice than white rice because it also has more fiber and more nutrients.

🐾 If you are out of a starch called for in a recipe, you can use crumbled whole wheat bread as a substitute. Use the heels of bread for breadcrumbs and keep frozen in baggies.

VEGETABLES

Vegetables are high in antioxidants and are very nutritious for your pet. In the recipes in this book, the vegetables can be canned, fresh or frozen. Some of the vegetables are best cooked in order to break down the cell walls because some vegetables are hard to digest for dogs. If using fresh vegetables, you can steam them or microwave them in a little water. The vegetables used in the recipes include zucchini, spinach, broccoli, carrots, green beans, peas, white potatoes, sweet potatoes, parsley, mixed vegetables, celery, lettuce and squash.

🐾 You can use fresh, canned or frozen vegetables interchangeably in all the recipes.

🐾 Chopped fresh parsley can be sprinkled on top of all the dishes.

🐾 Vegetables play an important role in the health of our dogs. Green vegetables heal at the cellular level through their antioxidant and anti-inflammatory properties.

🐾 Cabbage, Brussels sprouts and beans are not used in the recipes as they can cause severe gas.

DAIRY

Dairy is an important dietary ingredient for added calcium and flavor. The dairy products used in the following recipes are small curd cottage cheese, eggs, nonfat dry milk, sour cream, cream cheese, yogurt and all cheeses. The recipes calling for grated Parmesan cheese may be substituted with grated Romano cheese. The dishes calling for cheddar cheese in the following recipes may be substituted with Swiss, Mozzarella, Colby, or any other cheese you have on hand.

🐾 Packaged shredded cheese is usually always on sale. Stock up and freeze.

🐾 Eggs that are past their expiration date on the carton may still be used. Fill a bowl with water and place the eggs in it. If they float, throw them out. If they sink, they are still good to use.

🐾 Use the low-fat sour cream, cream cheese and yogurt if your dog tends to be overweight.

FOOD TIDBITS

🐾 All the recipes in this book use garlic powder. Garlic powder also comes mixed with parsley which is fine to use.

🐾 Use fold-top sandwich bags, which are much less expensive than the zip-lock bags to freeze leftovers for individual servings. If you place the bag in a glass, it makes it easier to fill rather than trying to hold it open. NEVER, EVER heat the food up in the plastic bag. Use a glass or paper plate to reheat leftovers on and cover with a paper towel. Do not cover with plastic wrap as it can melt down onto the food.

🐾 Rotate the recipes for a variety of the different nutrients that are in specific recipes.

🐾 Sprinkle wheat germ on top of the food for an excellent source of Vitamin E and Folic acid.

🐾 Organ meats and eggs are excellent sources of protein.

🐾 Shriveled potatoes, carrots, zucchini or other vegetables you have on hand (that we would normally throw out) are great in these recipes. Just make sure there are no green spots or mold on them.

🐾 If the leftover food becomes a little thick after refrigeration, add a little organic chicken or beef broth to it. The boxed variety of broths keeps very well in the refrigerator. If you use the canned broth and have leftover, pour the remaining broth into a glass jar and refrigerate.

🐾 Obesity is the number one health problem in all dogs today. Nearly one half of all dogs are overweight. A balanced diet is needed for the mental and physical health of your pet. Only you should control the food they eat.

🐾 If you have an overweight dog or a dog that has a low fat tolerance, tuna is very good for them because it is very low in fat. Make sure it is packed in water instead of oil to cut down on the fat content.

🐾 Meat protein is vital to your dog's health and promotes their healthy skin and coat. It also supports the immune and nervous systems. Plants have proteins but they are not complete and they are harder to digest. Puppies and older dogs require more protein in their diets.

🐾 Fruits can be fed to your pet if they like them. Some dogs love fruit and others don't. Just be sure that it is ripe.

🐾 Olive oil is used extensively in my recipes. You don't have to use the extra virgin olive oil for cooking. The light olive oil contains fewer calories and is less expensive.

🐾 Since cancer is the leading cause of death in dogs today, it is imperative that your dog eats vegetables, which are rich in carotenes. Vegetables contain chemicals called phytonutrients that have strong antioxidant properties. These help the liver with detoxification. These properties can also result in inhibiting tumor cell growth and stop cell death. They also keep your dog more active and staying young.

🐾 Water is a vital component of your pet's health. Make sure the water bowl is refreshed twice a day with bottled or filtered water. If you are not drinking tap water, why would you give it to your dog?

🐾 Fatty acids are vital to your pet's health. Omega-3 fatty acids are the ones that can help fight inflammation. Inflammation can cause arthritis, allergies, skin disease, kidney disease and heart disease. They may also help with some cancer tumors. These good acids can come from fish oil and flaxseed oil. You can also use a supplement that your veterinarian can recommend.

🐾 Be sure to clean the dog dish after each feeding.

🐾A carnivore is an animal that is strictly a meat eater. Dogs are omnivores, meaning they feed on both animals and plants. A diet of strictly meat would lead to a vitamin and mineral deficiency.

🐾The month of May has been declared "Cancer Awareness Month for Dogs."

🐾The most important news in health maintenance for your dog today is that better nutrition is the single, most important thing in preventing cancer.

🐾If you buy dry dog food, buy the organic variety, which is also low in fat. Dry food can have up to fifty percent more carbohydrates that the canned food. So look for brands that contain less than 9% fat content.

🐾Check with your veterinarian about giving your dog a vitamin and mineral supplement.

Here is a list of some common foods to **avoid**, as they may be toxic to your pet. Be sure to check with your veterinarian if you are feeding your dog something you are unsure of:

Mushrooms	Alcohol
Onions	Raw eggs
Yeast dough	Moldy foods
Grapes	Bones
Raisins	Sushi
Macadamia nuts	Mushrooms
Chocolate	Tea
Fruit pits	Candy
Coffee	Artificial Sweeteners
Tea	

RECIPE TIDBITS

The recipes in this chapter are made with five ingredients or less, with easy to follow instructions, and less expensive than most good quality dog food per pound. The reward for your time cooking will be a healthier dog and one who could live longer than the expected life span of his breed. This is beyond anything else you could do for your dog.

Elevated dog dishes that sit on stands are more comfortable for your pet. They don't have to bend over as far and they consume less air and gas while eating.

Eggshells contain valuable calcium. You can grind leftover eggshells very fine and add one teaspoon every other day to their food. You can grind them up in your blender or coffee grinder. Be sure and refrigerate the eggshells.

A homemade diet for dogs should consist of one-half protein, one-fourth carbohydrates, and one-fourth vegetables. The protein portion includes beef, turkey, lamb, organ meats, chicken, fish, eggs, cottage cheese, tuna, salmon, and mackerel.

Homemade food doesn't contain any preservatives so only refrigerate for up to three days and freeze for no longer than three months.

DOG TREATS

HEALTHY DOG TREATS

Treats are very important to your dog. They love it when you give them a treat for learning a new trick or they get a treat for a reward for something they have done. Or, you just want to give them a treat in the afternoon because you love them.

The dog treats in this book are simple and easy to make. Some are baked in the oven, some are cooked on top of the stove, and some require no baking or cooking at all.

Some food manufactures are making treats using "human-grade" ingredients. This means a human can eat them, as well as their dog. However, the price on these treats can be staggering.

Manufactured treats do not have to meet any nutrient standards. This means to the average consumer that they do not have to tell the calorie or sugar content, which can quickly add weight to a dog.

Remember the pet recall in 2007 of dog food and treats that were tainted with melamine from China and killed thousands of innocent dogs? You must be diligent and read labels if you are buying dog food and treats. But my feeling is that you will start making your own when you see how happy your dog is when he eats the treats that his master has made. Somehow, I believe, they know we made the treats just for them. Enjoy.

BAKED DOG TREATS

The following recipes are dog treats that require baking in the oven. Your dog will love the variety and you will feel good giving wholesome baked treats that are less expensive than store bought.

CRUNCHY EGGS

OATMEAL SQUARES

OVEN CHICKEN TENDERS

TURKEY CRUMBS

SWEET POTATO CHIPS

POTATO WEDGES

PEAR STICKS

BACON CORNBREAD

TURKEY CORNBREAD

BAKED APPLES

CRISPY CHICKEN CHIPS

SALMON AND DILL BISCUITS

MAMA'S MEATBALLS

PEANUT BUTTER BALLS

CRUNCHY EGGS

2 large eggs, whisked

2 slices bacon, cooked and crumbled

1 tablespoon grated Parmesan cheese

1 tablespoon oats, uncooked

Preheat oven to 350 degrees. Whisk the eggs in a bowl and crumble the bacon into the eggs. Add the cheese and oats. Pour mixture into a heated skillet with one-tablespoon olive oil until set, just like a pancake. Remove from the heat and cut into strips. Bake for about 20 minutes until crisp. Let cool and serve.

OATMEAL SQUARES

2 cups oats

1/2 cup oat flour

2 teaspoons baking powder

1/2 cup peanut butter, creamy

1/2 cup water

Preheat oven to 325 degrees. Mix together the oats, flour and baking powder. Mix the peanut butter and water in a separate bowl. Add the oat mixture to the peanut butter and water. Mix well and pour into an 8 x 8 greased baking pan. The batter will be fairly thick. Bake for 12-15 minutes. Turn off the oven and let the mixture cool inside the oven to crisp up. Cut into bite size squares for a healthy treat. Refrigerate any leftovers for up to three days.

OVEN CHICKEN TENDERS

1 package chicken tenders (2.5 pounds)

2 tablespoons olive oil

Preheat oven to 350 degrees. Grease a cookie sheet very well. Slice the tenders as thin as you can. Place the chicken tenders on the greased cookie sheet and also brush with olive oil on both sides. Bake for about 25-30 minutes until they are dried out. This is a wonderful and wholesome treat for your dog. Freeze in individual batches for a later treat.

🐾 Chicken breasts may also be substituted and sliced as thin as possible. Buy the chicken that is the least expensive per bag.

🐾🐾 Chicken thighs do not work with this recipe.

TURKEY CRUMBS

1 pound ground turkey

Preheat oven to 350 degrees. Brown the ground turkey in a skillet with one tablespoon olive oil and break up into medium pieces. Grease a cookie sheet and spread the turkey pieces out evenly. Cook for 15 minutes until crisp. Refrigerate for up to three days or freeze in plastic bags for a crunchy treat your dog will love.

🐾 Ground beef may also be used but the turkey crisps up better.

SWEET POTATO CHIPS

2 sweet potatoes, peeled and sliced

2 tablespoons olive oil

2 teaspoons grated Parmesan cheese

Preheat the oven to 325 degrees. Wash and peel the sweet potatoes. Slice into medium thick slices and then cut into quarters. Brush with olive oil and bake for 30 minutes stirring every 10 minutes until crisp. Remove from the oven and sprinkle with the Parmesan cheese. Let cool and store in airtight container for a great and healthy treat.

🐾 Grated Romano cheese may be substituted.

POTATO WEDGES

4 white medium potatoes, unpeeled and scrubbed

1 teaspoon garlic powder

2 tablespoons olive oil

Preheat oven to 375 degrees. Spray a cookie sheet. Pat the potatoes of all water. Cut the potatoes in half and then half again, making a wedge. Put the potatoes on the greased cookie sheet and sprinkle with the garlic powder and olive oil. Take your hands and toss the potatoes to get the garlic and olive oil on all sides. Bake for 20-25 minutes until crisp. Let cool and serve. Refrigerate any leftovers for up to five days.

PEAR STICKS

2 1/2 cups flour, whole wheat

2 large eggs, whisked

1 large pear, pureed

3 tablespoons canola oil

2 tablespoons molasses or maple syrup

Preheat oven to 350 degrees. Puree the pears in a food processor. Whisk the eggs, oil and molasses together. Add the pears and flour to this mixture and stir. Add one tablespoon of water at a time if the batter is too thick. Roll into five or six inch sticks. Place on a greased cookie sheet and bake for 15-20 minutes. These sticks will be crisp and make a wonderful treat your dog will love. Refrigerate any leftovers for up to three days.

Apples may be substituted for the pears.

BACON CORNBREAD

2 cups cornmeal, yellow or white

1 cup bacon, cooked and crumbled

1 garlic clove, chopped

2 large eggs, whisked

1 cup water

Preheat the oven to 375 degrees. Beat the eggs and add all the ingredients and mix well. Pour into a greased 8 x 8 pan and cook for 25-30 minutes. Let cool and cut into small squares. Refrigerate any leftovers for up to five days.

TURKEY CORNBREAD

1 pound ground turkey, uncooked

1 egg, whisked

1/3 cup milk

1 box corn muffin mix (8.5 ounce)

Preheat the oven to 400 degrees. Mix all the ingredients together and pour into a greased 8 x 8 glass or metal pan. Bake for 25-30 minutes. Let cool and cut into small squares. Refrigerate for up to three days.

BAKED APPLES

2 apples, sliced thin

2 tablespoons orange juice

1 teaspoon cinnamon

Preheat the oven to 350 degrees. Place the apples in a greased ovenproof dish and sprinkle with the orange juice and cinnamon. Bake for about 20 minutes and let cool before serving.

🐾 Pears can be substituted for the apples.

🐾🐾 If you don't want to turn the oven on, you can make these in a skillet until the apples are soft. Let cool before serving.

🐾🐾🐾 This can be doubled because your dog will love them.

CRISPY CHICKEN CHIPS

2 chicken breasts, cooked

1 cup oat flour

1/2 cup chicken broth

1 teaspoon garlic, chopped

1 teaspoon dried basil

Preheat the oven to 350 degrees. Puree the chicken, garlic and basil in a food processor until the chicken is chopped fine. In a bowl, mix the flour and chicken broth together. Add the chicken mixture and mix well. Drop by spoonfuls onto a greased cookie sheet and mash down with the bottom of a glass. Bake 25-30 minutes until brown. They will harden up for a delightful treat. Refrigerate any leftovers for up to three days.

Whole wheat or garbanzo flour can be substituted for the oat flour.

Dried parsley or oregano may be used in place of the basil.

SALMON & DILL BISCUITS

1 can (6 ounce) salmon, undrained

2 large eggs, whisked

1/2 cup flour, whole wheat

1 teaspoon dried dill

Preheat oven to 350 degrees. Whisk the eggs together in a bowl. Add the undrained salmon and break up. Then add the flour and dill to the mixture and mix well. Form into small balls and place on a greased cookie sheet. Cook for 18 minutes. Let cool and store in the refrigerator for up to three days or freeze for a later treat.

🐾 Any flour will work but preferably whole wheat or oat flour.

🐾🐾 You can substitute dried parsley for the dried dill.

MAMMA'S MEATBALLS

1 pound ground beef

1/2 cup bread crumbs

1 tablespoon Parmesan cheese, grated

1/2 cup water or broth

1/2 teaspoon garlic powder

Preheat oven to 350 degrees. Roll into tiny meatballs and place on a slightly greased cookie sheet. Bake for 20-25 minutes until browned. Let cool and serve as a treat. Refrigerate any leftovers for up to three days.

🐾 Ground turkey may also be used but turkey takes longer to bake. Increase the time to 30-35 minutes.

PEANUT BUTTER BALLS

4 cups flour, whole wheat

1 large egg, whisked

1 cup peanut butter, creamy

1 cup nonfat dried milk

3/4 cup warm water

Preheat oven to 350 degrees. Mix the warm water, peanut butter, and egg in a bowl. Add the flour a cup at a time until mixed well. Drop by spoonfuls onto a greased cookie sheet and bake for 25-30 minutes until brown. Let cool and the peanut balls will harden up for a great treat. Refrigerate any leftovers for up to five days.

NO BAKE DOG TREATS

The following recipes are dog treats that require no baking in the oven and very little cooking. Your dog will love the variety of these treats.

SHREDDED WHEAT BALLS

CHEERIOS BALLS

FROZEN BANANAS

FROZEN YOGURT

CHICKEN SAUCE

BBQ KIELBASA

WAFFLES

PUMPKIN YOGURT TREAT

BREAKFAST FEAST TREAT

LIVER DELIGHTS

EGGS AND TOAST

EGGS AND BACON

BEEF POPS

STEAK AND EGGS

SHREDDED WHEAT BALLS

1 cup shredded wheat, crushed

1/4 cup blue cheese, crumbled

2 ounces cream cheese

Crush the shredded wheat in a food processor. Add the blue cheese and cream cheese. Process this mixture until smooth. Roll into balls and serve. Refrigerate any leftovers for up to three days.

🐾 You can also crush the shredded wheat with a rolling pin in a zip-lock bag.

CHEERIOS BALLS

1 cup cheerios

1/4 cup peanut butter, creamy

2 ounces cream cheese

Mix the cheerios, peanut butter, and cream cheese in a bowl. Shape into small balls.

🐾 Use any cereal you have on hand but make sure it is not the sugared variety.

FROZEN BANANAS

4 ripe bananas, peeled and sliced

3 tablespoons peanut butter

Slice the bananas into medium slices and place on a cookie sheet. Freeze until the slices are slightly frozen. Spread the peanut butter on a slice and then top it with another slice for a "frozen sandwich" summertime treat. Freeze any remaining for a later treat.

FROZEN YOGURT

2 cups frozen yogurt, any flavor

1 banana, peeled and mashed

2 teaspoons peanut butter, creamy

1 teaspoon vanilla

Place the frozen yogurt into a bowl and let it come to room temperature, just until soft. Mash the banana with a fork and add it to the yogurt, along with the peanut butter and vanilla. Mix well and freeze. Give a tablespoon or two for a refreshing treat.

🐾 You can replace the vanilla with a teaspoon of honey.

CHICKEN SAUCE

3 chicken thighs, cooked

2 cups chicken broth

1 cup nonfat dried milk

2 large eggs, whisked

Boil the chicken thighs in the two cups of chicken broth. Let cool and then cut into pieces. Beat the eggs in a bowl along with the dried milk. Add the chicken pieces and any broth that was left from the pan. Place in a blender and process until smooth. Let cool and store in the refrigerator for up to three days. Freeze in an ice cube tray and let thaw to add flavor to any recipe or to organic dry dog food.

🐾 Heat the sauce slightly before using and skim any fat that has accumulated.

BBQ KIELBASA

1 package turkey kielbasa

1/4 cup BBQ sauce

Cut the kielbasa into small chucks. Place into a bowl and pour the BBQ sauce over and toss to coat. Give a few at a time for a treat. Refrigerate any leftovers for up to five days.

🐾 Be sure to cut into small chucks so your dog can eat them whole as not to cause a mess on the floor.

🐾🐾 Beef kielbasa may also be used.

WAFFLES

2 cups whole wheat flour

1/2 cup oats, uncooked

1 large egg, whisked

1 cup milk

1/4 cup peanut butter, creamy

Preheat a waffle iron and spray. Mix all the ingredients together except the peanut butter. Bake in the waffle iron until done. Spread a thin layer of peanut butter on each waffle and cut into pieces along the lines of the waffles. Let cool and serve as a treat. Refrigerate any leftovers for up to five days.

🐾 For extra sweetness, add a drizzle of maple syrup on top.

PUMPKIN-YOGURT TREAT

1 can (16 ounce) pumpkin

1/2 cup yogurt, vanilla

1/4 teaspoon cinnamon

Mix the pumpkin, yogurt, and cinnamon into a small bowl and mix well. Give about a half of a cup for a cool treat. Refrigerate any leftovers for up to five days.

🐾 My dogs love this and it's full of vitamins and fiber.

🐾 🐾 You can use nutmeg in place of the cinnamon or add both.

BREAKFAST FEAST TREAT

1 cup oatmeal, instant

1 banana, mashed

1 tablespoon peanut butter, creamy

1 teaspoon honey or maple syrup

Cook the oatmeal in the microwave as directed on the package with a little extra water. Let cool slightly and put in a bowl. Add the banana and peanut butter and mix well. Drizzle with the honey or maple syrup. Use as a treat and not as a meal replacement.

🐾 Use the creamy peanut butter and not the crunchy. Buy the less expensive organic store brand.

🐾 🐾 You can omit the honey or syrup if you don't have any on hand. But NEVER use sugar as a substitute for sweetness.

LIVER DELIGHTS

1 package chicken or beef livers (approximately one pound)

Put a tablespoon of olive oil in a skillet and fry the livers on medium heat sprinkled with a little garlic powder. This should take about 15 minutes and keep turning them until done. Let cool and cut into bite size pieces with kitchen shears for a special treat. Refrigerate any leftovers for up to three days.

🐾 Livers tend to burn quickly so keep on medium or even low heat. If they are starting to brown too fast before they are done, add a little water to the skillet.

EGGS AND TOAST

3 large eggs, whisked

4 slices bread, toasted whole wheat, cubed

4 ounces cream cheese

1/2 cup milk

1 teaspoon vanilla

Grease a skillet with 1 tablespoon olive oil. Cook the eggs until almost set. Add the cubed bread, cream cheese, milk and vanilla. Cook until the cream cheese has melted and the eggs are done. Let cool and serve as a breakfast treat.

BEEF POPS

1 can beef broth

1 cup water, bottled

Mix the broth and water together and pour into an ice cube tray and freeze for a summertime treat.

🐾 If your dog loves ice cubes, he will love these!

STEAK AND EGGS

2 cups leftover steak

2 large eggs, whisked

Leftover steak is great mixed with scrambled eggs for a nice treat. Save pieces of leftover steak in a zip-lock bag in the freezer and keep adding to it until you have about two cups. Thaw out the steak pieces. Put the eggs and steak pieces in a skillet with one tablespoon of olive oil. Scramble the eggs until done and let cool. Refrigerate any leftovers for up to three days.

🐾 Be sure to trim any fat and grizzle off the steak.

HERE IS A SAMPLING OF SOME NO-COOK TREATS YOU CAN GIVE TO YOUR DOG:

POPCORN, PLAIN AND UNSALTED

CHEESE CUBES

HOTDOGS, TURKEY OR BEEF, SLICED

YOGURT, ANY FLAVOR

SHERBET, ANY FLAVOR

COTTAGE CHEESE, SMALL CURD

CEREAL, UNSWEETENED

CELERY

CARROTS

CANTALOUPE PIECES

WATERMELON, SEEDLESS

BANANAS, SLICED

APPLES, SLICED

PEARS, SLICED

ZUCCHINI, UNCOOKED STRIPS

PEANUTS, UNSALTED

JICAMA, SLICED

RICE CAKE PIECES

DOG RECIPES

CUBED STEAK

BEEFY/BARKY STEW

ROLLOVER LEFTOVERS

SHEPHERD'S PIE

TURKEY & NOODLES

CHICKEN LIVERS AND GIZZARDS

CHICKEN AND LIVER PATÉ

TURKEY AND RICE

SALMON PATTY

CHICKEN/BARLEY STEW

ITALIAN GOULASH

EGGS BENEDICT

POTATO & EGG SCRAMBLE

BBQ DINNER

SARDINES PLEASE

TUNA SALAD

SWEET SALMON

SALMON STEW

TUNA SALAD

SKILLET TUNA

BLUE PLATE SPECIAL

CRANBERRY TURKEY

CHICKEN STROGANOFF

MEAT LOAF

TUNA CAKES

TURKEY BURGERS

GOULASH

SUNDAY CHICKEN

APPLE DELIGHT

CHICKEN STRATA

HOUND HASH

HAWAIIAN DINNER

CUBED STEAK

2 cubed steaks, tenderized

1/2 cup cottage cheese, small curd

1/2 cup whole wheat elbow macaroni, cooked

1 box frozen chopped spinach, cooked and drained (or one 15 oz can, drained)

In a skillet, add a little olive oil and brown the steaks over medium heat on both sides until done. They cook quickly so it will only take a few minutes on both sides. There will be little fat as the cubed steaks are lean, so just add a little water to scrap up the brown bits and then turn off the burner. Remove the steaks from the skillet and use kitchen shears to cut into pieces. Return the steaks to the skillet and add the cottage cheese, the cooked macaroni and the drained spinach. Mix well and cool before serving. Refrigerate any leftovers for up to three days.

🐾 The tenderized steaks cook very quickly.

🐾 🐾 Use any frozen vegetable that your dog likes. You will get to know the vegetables your dog likes and dislikes.

🐾 🐾 🐾 Cook up a whole box of elbow macaroni and keep it covered in the refrigerator to use for the week. You can substitute cooked egg noodles or potatoes for the macaroni.

BEEFY/BARKY STEW

1 boneless chuck roast (about 3 pounds)

3 diced potatoes, uncooked and unpeeled

1 small bunch broccoli, cut-up, stalks included

1 cup beef broth

Place the roast in a crock-pot and sprinkle with garlic powder. Add the broth and cook for four to five hours. Add the diced potatoes and broccoli to the crock-pot the last hour of cooking. Remove the roast, potatoes and broccoli from the crock-pot and let cool. Shred the roast and then mix in the potatoes and broccoli. Add some of the broth from the crock-pot to this mixture and serve. Refrigerate any leftover broth and use it in other recipes that call for beef broth. Skim the fat off the top before using. Refrigerate any leftovers for up to three days.

🐾 This will make enough for several meals. You can keep adding leftover vegetables or potatoes from other meals, if needed.

🐾 🐾 Remove the leaves from the broccoli. Cut up the stalks but leave the broccoli in bunches so they don't fall apart while cooking.

🐾 🐾 🐾 As always, you can substitute any vegetable for the broccoli. Carrots would work well also.

ROLLOVER LEFTOVERS

2 cups leftover turkey, diced or shredded

1/2 cup instant oatmeal, cooked

1/2 cup carrots, uncooked and shredded

1/3 cup chicken broth

1 tablespoon grated Parmesan cheese

Shred or dice the turkey or chicken and place in a bowl. Cook the oatmeal in the microwave and let it cool slightly. Process the carrots in the food processor. Add the oatmeal, carrots, broth and cheese to the turkey or chicken and mix well. Refrigerate any leftovers for up to three days.

🐾 Process a bag of carrots all at once in the food processor and store in the refrigerator in a zip-lock bag. They will keep for weeks and you will always have some on hand.

🐾 🐾 Keep a box of chicken broth, preferably organic and low fat, in the refrigerator for the whole week.

🐾 🐾 🐾 Cook the oatmeal in a little more water than called for on the directions and it won't come out as thick. You can add more water, if needed.

SHEPHERD'S PIE

1 pound ground beef

1 cup mashed potatoes, leftover, fresh, or instant

2 large eggs, whisked

1 (15 ounce) can green beans, undrained

Heat a skillet with one tablespoon olive oil. Brown the ground beef and drain the grease off. Add the eggs in with the beef and cook until set. Turn off the heat and add the potatoes and undrained green beans. Mix and let cool. Refrigerate any leftovers for up to three days.

🐾 No leftover potatoes and no time to cook fresh ones? You can use instant mashed potatoes. Make a batch to have on hand and keep refrigerated.

🐾 🐾 Cut the green beans up with kitchen shears while still in the can. They are easier to eat for the smaller dogs. If you buy the French-cut beans, they are already smaller in size and no need to cut them up. You may also use frozen, as well, or substitute any other green vegetable in this recipe.

TURKEY & NOODLES

1 pound ground turkey

1 cup cooked egg noodles, small width

1 (15 ounce) cans peas, drained

1/2 cup chicken broth

Brown the turkey in a skillet in a tablespoon of olive oil. No need to drain as there will be little fat. Turn off the heat and add the cooked noodles, peas and chicken broth with the turkey and mix well. Let cool and serve. Refrigerate any leftovers for up to three days.

🐾 Grocery stores usually have the ground turkey marked down in the mornings and in the evenings. Stock up and freeze when you get a good deal. Ground chicken may also be used.

🐾 🐾 Dogs love egg noodles. Look for the smaller width and whole wheat variety. They also come in a package called fine noodles. Sometimes they are hard to find but they cook up in a few minutes.

🐾 🐾 🐾 My dogs happen to love peas but you can certainly use any vegetable in this recipe.

CHICKEN LIVERS AND GIZZARDS

1 package chicken livers gizzards (approximately one pound)

1 cup cooked instant brown rice

1 cup grated zucchini uncooked, unpeeled

1/2 cup chicken broth

Boil the chicken gizzards in a pan of water sprinkled with garlic powder. These will take about 20 minutes to cook. Drain and cut up the gizzards with kitchen shears and put in a small bowl. Add the cooked instant brown rice and the grated zucchini. Mix in the chicken broth and serve when cool. Refrigerate for up to three days.

🐾 This is also good with grated carrots.

🐾 🐾 Dogs love the organ meats and they are very good for them. Limit organ meat meals to once or twice a week, as they are very rich and can cause diarrhea.

CHICKEN AND LIVER PATÉ

1/2 cup chicken thighs, cooked

1/2 cup chicken livers, cooked

1/2 cup zucchini, uncooked, unpeeled, shredded

1 teaspoon Parmesan cheese

Shred the chicken and cut the livers into small pieces. Shred the zucchini in a food processor along with the Parmesan cheese. Place the chicken and livers in a bowl. Add the zucchini and Parmesan cheese and mix well. Refrigerate for up to three days.

🐾 Cook up a whole chicken or package of thighs to have on hand for the week.

🐾🐾 Shred a whole zucchini or two at a time and keep refrigerated.

🐾🐾🐾 Add some garlic powder to the water the livers cook in.

TURKEY AND RICE

1 pound ground turkey

1 cup cooked instant brown rice

1 cup cooked broccoli

1/2 cup chicken broth

Brown the turkey in a tablespoon of olive oil. There is no need to drain as there will be little fat. Turn off the heat and add the rice and broccoli to the skillet. Then add the chicken broth and mix well. Let cool and serve. Refrigerate any leftovers for up to three days.

🐾 Ground chicken may also be used.

🐾 🐾 Instant brown rice comes in either individual bags or in full boxes. The instant cooks up in about 10 minutes in the microwave. This is a real time saver.

🐾 🐾 🐾 You can use fresh or frozen broccoli. Keep a bag of frozen in your freezer at all times, and just take out what you need.

SALMON PATTY

1 (6 ounce) can salmon, drained

1/2 cup mashed potatoes

1/4 cup beef broth

2 tablespoons cottage cheese, small curd

1 tablespoon parsley

Mix all the ingredients together in a bowl. Heat a skillet with one tablespoon olive oil. Form into patties and fry on both sides until crisp. Cut into pieces and serve. Refrigerate any leftovers for up to two days.

🐾 Since everything is cooked in this recipe, you only need to brown the patties briefly.

🐾 🐾 Use leftover potatoes or instant.

🐾 🐾 Grate 2 tablespoons carrots or zucchini in place of the cottage cheese.

CHICKEN/BARLEY STEW

6 chicken thighs

1 cup barley

1 can mixed vegetables, undrained

1/2 cup chicken broth, from pan

Boil the chicken and barley together for about 25 minutes until done. Reserve the liquid. Remove the skin and bone from the thighs and shred with a fork into a bowl. Add the cooked barley, vegetables, and the chicken broth from the pan. Mix well and serve when cool. Refrigerate any leftovers for up to three days.

🐾 White chicken meat cooks faster than dark chicken meat.

🐾🐾 A cup of frozen mixed vegetables may be used in place of the canned vegetables.

ITALIAN GOULASH

1 pound ground beef

2 cups cooked elbow macaroni

1 (15 ounce) cans peas, undrained

1 tomato, diced

2 tablespoons grated Parmesan cheese

Cook the ground beef in an ungreased skillet and drain any grease that is in the skillet. Add the beef back into the skillet and add the macaroni, peas, tomato and Parmesan cheese and mix well. Let cool and serve. Refrigerate any leftovers for up to three days.

🐾 Use any pasta that you have on hand if you don't have the elbow macaroni.

EGGS BENEDICT

4 large eggs, whisked

2 slices bacon, cooked and crumbled

1 cup spinach, canned or frozen

1/2 cup sour cream

Cook the bacon in a skillet until crisp and drain on paper towels. Let cool and crumble or cut into small dice. Wipe the skillet of all bacon grease and cook the eggs until set. Turn off the heat and add the bacon, spinach and sour cream. Stir and let cool. Refrigerate any leftovers for up to three days.

🐾 Keep some cooked bacon in the freezer at all times for a quick addition.

🐾 🐾 This recipe can be served for breakfast or dinner.

POTATO & EGG SCRAMBLE

4 large eggs, whisked

1 medium potato, cooked and diced

1/2 cup cottage cheese

1 teaspoon dried parsley

Scramble the eggs in a skillet with a teaspoon of olive oil. Turn off the heat and add the potato, cottage cheese and parsley. Let cool and serve. Refrigerate any leftovers for up to three days.

🐾 Any leftover potatoes will work with this recipe. You can use leftover mashed, scalloped or a baking potato.

BBQ DINNER

2 pounds beef stew meat

2 cups cooked egg noodles, small width

1 can (15 ounce) peas, drained

1/2 cup sour cream

3 tablespoons BBQ sauce

Cook the beef stew meat in a skillet with a teaspoon of olive oil until done. Cook the noodles while the beef is cooking and drain. Turn off the heat and drain the excess grease from the beef cubes. Add the egg noodles, peas, sour cream and BBQ sauce. Stir and let cool. Refrigerate any leftovers for up to three days.

🐾 Fine egg noodles are very thin and cook quickly.

🐾 🐾 Dogs love the taste of BBQ sauce; but be sure it is not the spicy variety.

SARDINES PLEASE

1 cans sardines, drained

1 cup cooked egg noodles, small width

1 can (15 ounces) sliced carrots, drained

1/2 cup plain yogurt

Place the drained sardines into a bowl. Add the noodles, carrots, and the yogurt. Mix well and serve. Refrigerate any leftovers for up to two days.

 This is a very rich meal. Serve sardines no more than once a week.

TUNA SALAD

1 can (6 ounce) tuna, packed in water and drained

1/2 cup chopped spinach, fresh or frozen

1/2 cup lettuce, shredded

1/2 cup peaches, fresh, frozen or canned

1/2 cup carrots, shredded, uncooked

Drain the tuna and put into a bowl. Add the spinach, lettuce, peaches and carrots. Mix well and serve. Refrigerate any leftovers for up to two days.

🐾 Cut the peaches into small pieces.

🐾 🐾 The carrots may be raw or cooked.

SWEET SALMON

1 can (16 ounce) salmon, drained

1 sweet potato, cooked and diced

1 cup frozen peas, (defrosted) or canned

1/2 cup cottage cheese, small curd

Place the drained salmon into a bowl and mix in the potato, peas and cottage cheese. Serve at once. Refrigerate any leftovers for up to two days.

🐾 Great on a summer day as no cooking is involved.

🐾 🐾 Microwave the sweet potato and dice. Or you can use frozen sweet potato fries and cut them into bite size pieces.

SALMON STEW

1 can (16 ounce) salmon, drained

1 cup elbow macaroni, cooked

1 cup zucchini, shredded, uncooked

1/2 cup carrots, shredded, uncooked

Drain the salmon into a bowl and break up. Add the macaroni, zucchini and carrots. Mix well and serve. Refrigerate any leftovers for up to two days.

🐾 This is a great summertime meal. All you have to cook is the macaroni unless you have some already cooked and ready in the refrigerator.

🐾🐾 Any assortment of vegetables may be used.

TUNA SALAD

1 can (6 ounce) tuna, packed in water, and drained

1 cup shredded lettuce

1/2 cup carrots, shredded

1/2 cup celery, diced

2 tablespoons cheddar cheese, shredded

Place the drained tuna in a bowl. Add the lettuce, carrots, celery and cheese. Mix well and serve. Refrigerate any leftovers for up to three days.

🐾 Another great summertime no-cook meal.

SKILLET TUNA

1 can (6 ounce) tuna, drained

1 cup mashed potatoes, leftover or instant

1 can (15 ounce) peas and carrots, drained

1/4 cup sour cream

1/4 cup shredded cheddar cheese

Heat a skillet with one tablespoon olive oil. Add the tuna, potatoes, peas and carrots, sour cream and cheddar cheese. Heat until cheese melts. Let cool and serve. Refrigerate any leftovers for up to three days.

🐾 Cottage cheese may also be substituted for the sour cream.

BLUE PLATE SPECIAL

2 cups cooked turkey, diced

1 cup mashed potato, leftover or instant

1 cup sweet potato, cooked and diced

1 can (15 ounce) peas, drained

1 cup chicken broth

Mix all the ingredients together and serve. Refrigerate any leftovers for up to three days.

🐾 Microwave the sweet potato, let cool and dice into pieces.

CRANBERRY TURKEY

2 cups cooked turkey, diced

1 cup cooked egg noodles, small width

1/2 cup cranberry, jellied

1/2 cup green beans, drained

1/2 cup peas and carrots, drained

Place the diced turkey in a bowl. Add the egg noodles, cranberry, green beans and peas and carrots. Mix well and serve. Refrigerate any leftovers for up to three days.

🐾 This is a no-cook meal that your dog will love.

🐾 🐾 Cook up a whole bag of egg noodles and keep in the refrigerator to use all week.

CHICKEN STROGANOFF

3 chicken breasts, diced

1 box frozen spinach, chopped

1/2 cup sour cream

1/2 cup chicken broth

Fry the chicken in 2 tablespoons olive oil. Defrost the spinach in the microwave and squeeze dry. Cut the chicken into cubes after cooling. Add the chicken back into the skillet; add the spinach, sour cream and chicken broth. Let cool and serve. Refrigerate any leftovers for up to three days.

🐾 Plain yogurt may be substituted for the sour cream.

MEAT LOAF

1 pound ground beef

1 large egg, whisked

2 peeled carrots, shredded

1/2 cup cooked brown rice

1/2 cup beef broth

Preheat the oven to 375 degrees. Mix all the ingredients together in a bowl. Place the mixture into a pan and shape into a meatloaf. Cook for 30-40 minutes until done. Let cool and cut into pieces. Refrigerate any leftovers for up to three days.

🐾 You can replace the brown rice with breadcrumbs, preferably with whole wheat bread.

🐾 🐾 If you don't have beef broth on hand, milk may be substituted.

TUNA CAKES

1 can (six ounce) tuna, drained, packed in water

1 large egg, whisked

1 slice whole wheat bread, crumbled

1/2 cup mixed vegetables, canned or frozen

1/4 cup chicken broth

Mix all the ingredients in a bowl. Heat a skillet with one tablespoon olive oil. Shape into small patties and fry on both sides until brown. Cool and serve. Refrigerate any leftovers for up to three days.

🐾 Process the bread in a food processor to make the breadcrumbs or use breadcrumbs that you have on hand.

TURKEY BURGERS

4 turkey burgers

1 cup elbow macaroni, cooked

1 can (15 ounce) green beans, drained

2 tablespoons BBQ sauce

1 tablespoon dried parsley

Cook the turkey burgers in a skillet with 2 tablespoon olive oil. Turn off the heat and let cool to the touch. Cut into bite size pieces with kitchen shears. Add the macaroni, green beans, BBQ sauce and parsley to the skillet. Mix well and serve.

🐾 Do not drain the oil in the skillet. There will be little fat from the turkey burgers and the olive oil that is left in the pan is good for them.

🐾 🐾 Broccoli works well with this dish in place of the green beans.

🐾 🐾 🐾 Parsley can be dried or fresh, or omitted if none on hand.

GOULASH

1 pound ground beef

2 cups egg noodles, cooked, small width

1 can green beans, drained

1 cans carrots, drained

1/2 cup cottage cheese, small curd

Brown the ground beef in a skillet with one tablespoon olive oil. Drain any grease from the skillet and wipe clean. Turn off the heat and add the noodles, green beans, carrots and cottage cheese. Let cool and serve. Refrigerate any leftovers for up to three days.

🐾 Any leftover potatoes may be substituted for the noodles.

SUNDAY CHICKEN

2 cups chicken, cooked and diced

2 cups cooked egg noodles, small width

1 can (15 ounce) peas and carrots, drained

1 can (15 ounce) chicken broth

Cook the noodles in with the can of chicken broth mixed with one cup of water. Put the chicken into a bowl. Add the noodles and the peas and carrots. Let cool and serve. Refrigerate any leftovers for up to three days.

🐾 Green beans are good in this recipe. You can add them as an additional ingredient or to replace the peas and carrots.

APPLE DELIGHT

1 pound ground beef

1 cup applesauce

1 cup brown rice, cooked

1 cup potatoes, cooked and diced

1 can (16 ounces) green beans, drained

Brown the ground beef in a skillet with one tablespoon olive oil. Drain the beef and wipe the skillet clean. Turn off the heat and add the applesauce, brown rice, potatoes and green beans. Let cool and serve. Refrigerate any leftovers for up to three days.

CHICKEN STRATA

4 chicken thighs, cooked and diced

1 medium baked potato, diced

1 zucchini, unpeeled, small dice

1/4 cup sour cream

2 tablespoons grated Parmesan cheese

Put the zucchini in a skillet with two tablespoons olive oil. Cook the zucchini until slightly done. Add the chicken, potato and sour cream to the skillet. Mix well and let cool. Before serving, sprinkle with the Parmesan cheese. Refrigerate any leftovers for up to three days.

🐾 The chicken thighs may be cooked in the microwave on high setting until they are done and then dice them when cooled.

HOUND HASH

2 pounds stew meat

1 cup cooked brown rice

1 can (15 ounces) pears, drained and diced

1 can green beans, drained

1/2 cup beef broth

Cook the stew meat in a skillet with two tablespoons olive oil. Turn off the heat and add the rice, pears, green beans and broth. Mix well and let cool before serving. Refrigerate any leftovers for up to three days.

🐾 Cut the stew meat into smaller pieces if they are too large.

HAWAIIAN DINNER

2 cups cooked chicken, diced

1 sweet potato, cooked and diced

1/2 cup cantaloupe, diced

1/2 cup carrots, uncooked and shredded

1/2 cup cottage cheese, small curd

For a no-cook meal, use leftover chicken and microwave the sweet potato and dice. Put into a bowl and add the cantaloupe, carrots and cottage cheese. Refrigerate any leftovers for up to three days.

🐾 You can substitute diced apple in place of the cantaloupe.

🐾🐾 Another great summertime no-cook meal.

Dog Section
III

FUN FACTS

The fastest dog is the Greyhound which can reach speeds of over 40 mph.

The pads on a dog's foot will insure a good grip when he jumps.

Dogs are found on every continent.

A female dog with pups passes immunity onto them through the antibodies that are present in her milk.

A dog can fully widen the pupils in their eyes in order to have better night vision.

Wonder why a male dog cocks his leg when eliminating? They want to mark their scent so profoundly to other dogs that they mark it as close to their nose level as possible.

Wonder why your dog's ears move around when you talk to them or they hear a sound? They are moving the muscles in their ears to focus the noise inward and funnel the sound waves into their ears.

A Chow Chow has a bluish-black tongue and gums. The tongue and gums are pink at birth and then turn dark by about eight weeks old.

A Newfoundland has webbed feet which makes them great swimmers.

Not all dogs can swim. A Basset Hound can't swim because their legs are too short to keep them afloat.

Dogs discharge their body heat by panting and they sweat from the bottoms of their feet.

If your dog is contented, he will usually yawn frequently.

The membranes inside a dog's nose, if unfolded and laid out, would be larger than the dog itself. This makes dogs one of the keenest animals for smell.

Way back when, people used to put their little dogs under the covers. They believed that if there were fleas and bedbugs in the bed that they would jump onto the dog and not on them.

VELCRO ® was invented by a Swiss inventor in the 1940s. He was walking his dog through the woods and when he returned home, his dog and his pants were covered with cockle burrs. He could hardly get them off his dog and his pants and was curious why they were so stubborn to remove. He examined them under a microscope and saw that they had a stiff hook shape that had attached themselves to the fur on his dog and his pants.

A smile from you to a strange dog may mean that you are baring your teeth for a fight with him.

In the Titanic disaster, very few people thought that the ship would sink. In the early boarding of the lifeboats, people didn't rush to them. A woman from New York boarded the lifeboat with her Pomeranian and Mr. Harper (from the famous publishing family) brought his Pekingese on board. And yes, they all did survive.

The expression "Three Dog Night" came into being because of the Nomadic people. They needed at least three dogs to keep them from freezing on cold nights in the wild.

The Irish Wolf hound is so strong that he can pick up another dog by the back of the neck and shake them to death when in a fight.

Dalmatians are born white and then develop their black spots.

The Bloodhound was named after an aristocrat and not because he smells the blood of a missing person.

The Afghan hound was a favorite dog of royalty and the name literally means "monkey-faced hound."

The Boxer stands on his front paws when he fights, which makes him look like a boxer in the ring.

A one year old dog is as mature as a fifteen year old person.

The puppy love we feel for our new pet is the beginning of an affair that lasts a lifetime.

Anyone can purchase a dog - but it takes an OWNER to set the tail wagging.

A puppy is interested not in food, but playing. An older dog is not interested in playing, but lives for food.

How did the expression "dumb dog" come about? Who is out working all day and who is sleeping the day away?

Your dog is loyal to you not because you feed it but because of the comfort and the companionship you provide to it.

Put a sweater on your short-haired dog when you take him out for a winter walk.

Never wake a sleeping dog by shaking or poking at it.

Always say your dog's name before you give it a command.

One in every three families in the United States owns one or more dogs.

Choke chains can be dangerous to your dog.

The Basenji, an African wolf, is the only dog that can't bark.

The Girl Scouts, Boy Scouts and the 4-H Clubs all offer merit badges in dog care.

The oldest age recorded for a dog was 29 years. It was a Queensland Heeler named Bluey, who lived in Australia. The average age for that breed is 15 years old.

Many foot disorders in dogs are related to long toenails, so have them checked and trimmed regularly.

The normal body temperature of a dog is 101.2 degrees.

Your dog is your true friend. You can be certain that he will never "talk" about you, no matter what you do.

The average dog lives to be 8 to 15 years.

If you leave your television on during the day, your dog won't howl.

Let's learn from our dog by being faithful, by being compassionate and by always being there.

One who says, "I work like a dog", evidently doesn't own one.

If you crate your dog while you are away at work, be sure to keep it clean. A great way to clean a crate is to take it to a self-serve car wash and blast it clean.

Why don't dogs get hairballs like cats do if they also lick themselves? It is because they have smooth tongues and the hair doesn't adhere to it.

New Jersey is trying to pass legislation to change the taste of antifreeze to make it less appealing to dogs. Antifreeze is toxic to dogs if they ingest it.

Cynology means the study of dogs. Kyon is the Greek word for dog, and logos is the Greek word for knowledge.

Of all the mammals, dogs have the greatest variation of sizes and shapes of any other mammal.

The skeleton of a dog has 319 bones, which is almost 100 more bones than that of a human skeleton.

Do you ever wonder why your dog can destroy their toys to shreds? The upper and lower teeth work like scissors which shreds the toys apart. This scissor action also aids them in pulling the flesh off a bone.

The gestation period for a dog is 59 to 66 days. If the pups are born earlier than 57 days, they cannot survive, unlike human babies that can sometimes survive a premature birth.

The spots on a dog's tongue are extra pigments, much like those resembling human freckles.

California holds an annual Ugliest Dog Competition. For three times in a row, a Chinese dog that is bald, has warts all over its body, buck teeth, white eyes and stray hairs on the top of its head has won the competition.

The Golden Retriever is used to help the physically disabled. They are trained to work with wheelchairs, to open doors and to pick up objects his master has dropped on the floor and cannot reach.

The medical profession is aware that dog owners are sick less often and suffer less severe health problems. Petting your dog can help lower blood pressure.

Cross breeds of the Cocker Spaniels and Poodles are used quite often for the physically disabled that were born deaf.

During a baseball game between the Los Angeles Dodgers and the Cincinnati Reds, a college student went onto the field with his dog and proceeded to play Frisbee. His dog was jumping up to nine feet into the air to catch the Frisbee. This was the start of a favorite sport between a man and his dog and also gave way to competition events featuring Frisbee-catching.

Larger dogs age more quickly than smaller dogs.

Exercise is so important to dogs and more important to specific breeds. If you own a dog in the herding group, it needs to run. If you own a dog in the sporting group, he likes to play catch and fetch.

If you can't devote time to walking your dog and exercising him with games, consider having a second dog so that they can provide the exercise they need by playing with each other.

Dogs are overweight much more than they are underweight. Overeating is as much as a problem for dogs as it is for humans. If your dog is overweight; change his diet, feed him less and exercise him more. He depends on you for his health.

When you give a command to your dog, always stand up straight and voice your command while looking down at him. Once he obeys, get down to his level and give him a treat while you are praising him.

If your dog suffers anxiety while you are away, they can become very destructive to your house and belongings in order to "pass the time." If you come home to a mess, still praise your dog and it will help to relieve his anxiety. Humans can always "pass the time" by talking on the phone, watching television, listening and dancing to music, surfing the web, reading, gardening, etc. What distraction does your dog have? YOU. They depend on you, so make their life as pleasant as you can.

There are only four U.S. cities that allow leashed dogs on public transportation that are not seeing-eye dogs. They are Boston, Toronto, Seattle and San Francisco. In Europe, however, nearly all the city transportation will allow leashed dogs.

Do you wonder why your dog goes in circles sometimes before he lays down? Wild dogs used to go in circles to flatten the grass to make their beds at night.

The heaviest dog recorded was an Old English Mastiff who weighed over 300 pounds.

Be a responsible pet owner to your neighbor. Clean up after your dog, abide by the leash law and make sure he is not disturbing your neighbors by barking.

The sense of touch has a strong affect on your dog. You can massage your dog by starting at the head and working down the body using circular moves. Your dog will love this and it may also reduce bad dog behavior and create a bond between you and your dog.

Although dogs love to be touched and petted, most do not like to be hugged. Your dog may feel this as very confining and restricting. When you hug your dog, you are immobilizing him. He may struggle to get away because the freedom of movement was so important for his survival when he was out in the wild. His survival was either to defend himself or run away from the threat.

The most common reason that dogs are put in shelters by their owners is usually because of their erratic behavior. A healthy diet full of vitamins and minerals can calm a dog and sometimes behavior problems are a result of a poor diet.

Dogs have fewer taste buds on their tongues than humans have, which enables them to eat almost anything. But nature is on their side. If the have eaten anything that is toxic, the body rejects the food by vomiting it up.

Why don't dogs get cavities like humans? Mainly because they don't eat sugar and their teeth do not have any pits or grooves in them like human teeth. The teeth are smooth and food cannot get trapped and cause decay.

The reason dogs can swallow bones and toys is because their esophagus is very elastic, allowing an object to enter into the esophagus very easily and get trapped. *WARNING* Do not give your dog small bones or toys to chew on.

Do you think your dog has a belly button? If you answered yes, you are right! Dogs are mammals that have developed inside their mother. They are attached by an umbilical cord that connects them to the mother. Even though they are born in a sac, the cord is attached to the mother until she bites it off after birth. Look closely and you'll find it on your dog's stomach.

The word dog-napper was coined when thieves stole the dogs of royalty for ransom.

Henry Bergh, the son of a New York ship builder, formed the American Society for the Prevention of Cruelty to Animals in the 1800s. Then in the late 1800s, Mr. Bergh also helped to develop the Child Welfare Society.

Does your dog eat grass at every opportunity? Maybe he is just smelling and tasting it to see if other dogs have been around. On the other hand, if he is eating grass, he could have an upset stomach. The grass will bind to the food that is making them sick so they can vomit it up. Or, maybe they just like the taste of it.

If your dog licks himself, it could be a sign of boredom. If they lick a person, they are gathering information about them. It is also a sign of affection for his master. Notice that he will always wag his tail while he is licking you. Also, the skin is the largest organ and he could be licking himself to get rid of waste and chemicals that are on his body.

It is said that a dog's mouth is cleaner that a human's. Why is that? When they lick their wounds, the wound seems to heal faster. What is really happening though is that by licking the wound, they are stimulating the blood flow to that area. They are also licking off the dead tissues that are on the wound and helps to promote faster healing.

Bones can cause your dog's teeth to fracture and injure their internal organs when they swallow the bone splinters. If you do give your dog bones, beef bones are the best. Never give chicken bones or rib bones because these bones tend to splinter easily.

If dogs could eat only meat, they would. But that would lead to vitamin and mineral deficiencies.

Do you think you look like your dog? There are no scientific studies that have been done on this but there is a theory. Since we are all so familiar with our own faces, it may be that when we go to pick out our dog, we tend to pick the dog that looks something like our own face.

Remember Lassie? Lassie was introduced in 1943. All the collies that played Lassie have been male dogs. The reason is that male collies usually have thicker coats, which on camera looked better than the thinner coats that female collies have.

There have been many Lassies through the years and they all had to have several things in common. They all had to have four white feet, a white stripe down their nose and a white collar around their head. The collies were bred a bit larger than the standard collies, so that as the child actors grew up and got taller, it was less noticeable to the audience.

Dance with your dog and they will dance with you...even without music.

Sing to your dog and they will feel your love for them...and maybe join in with a howl or two.

Laugh out loud while looking at your dog...and he will silently laugh with you.

The first formal seeing-eye dog training for the blind was established in 1929.

In the September 11th tragedy, a Golden Retriever guided his blind master down more than seventy flights of stairs to safety. At one time, the owner took the harness off of his dog and told him to go. In the intense heat and smoke, the dog stayed with his master, nudging him step by step down to safety. He was later honored for heroism and received a medal for the dedication to his master.

Dog therapy has had amazing results with humans. People who have not talked for years respond to a dog and will talk to it. Dogs open up an avenue for the patient to relate to the dog, which in turn, helps them then relate to their families and to their doctor.

Dogs are also used in mental institutions and nursing homes for touch therapy. Touch is the most underrated human sense that we relate to. Patients respond to being touched by the dog and then they learn to touch and pet the dog in return.

Therapy dogs also include seeing-eye dogs for the blind. German Shepherds were trained after WWI to help the servicemen who were blinded in combat. Although German Shepherds are still used today, Golden Retrievers and Labrador Retrievers are also used extensively. A new breed, the Lab/Golden, is a cross between the Labrador Retrievers and the Golden Retrievers, and they are also being used to lead the blind.

Dogs can understand hundreds of words but not whole sentences.

Dogs can also understand our gestures. If you point at something, your dog will look at where you are pointing.

A mother dog knows the different sounds for each of her puppies. Dogs communicate with humans by growling, howling, baying, whining, barking, yipping and yelping. As their master, you will also start to recognize each sound your dog makes, just like the mother and her puppies.

Dogs can remember a word for up to two minutes. But don't repeat yourself, as commands should be said just one time for the maximum effect.

Keep your voice commands short and distinct and your dog will understand you better.

Dogs don't understand our human language so you need to teach them. You also need to understand theirs. Training strengthens the bond between the dog and his master, as trust and respect are learned on both sides.

Training can begin as early as six weeks and up. Older dogs can also learn very quickly, contrary to the saying "you can't teach an old dog a new trick."

It wasn't until the late 1960's that the concept of dogs being trained to detect narcotics and contraband was implemented. Dogs have been trained to sniff out explosives, heroin, cocaine, people, marijuana and produce. They are used extensively in airports today to sniff out cargo and luggage for explosives.

Smell is the most advanced sense a dog has, and it comprises the biggest part of their brain. Dogs actually communicate with other dogs through their sense of smell.

Why do dogs have wet noses? It helps to bring the molecules that are in the air into contact with the wet nose and to help inhale the smell into their olfactory membrane.

The olfactory membrane in dogs is around 20 square inches versus 1/2 square inch in humans. Inside this membrane are sensory cells .Humans have around 5 million of these cells and dogs have up to 200 million, depending on the breed. This is why dogs are used to sniff out gas leaks that humans can't smell and to sniff out the truffles that grow underground.

Only eels smell better than dogs do.

The intelligence of a dog is usually measured by how quickly they learn a command quickly and to solve problems. A few of the most intelligent breeds are:

Border Collies   Golden Retrievers
Poodles   Dobermans
German Shepherds   Labradors
                                Rottweilers

DOG NAMES

Since dogs have become "family members", the names have changed over the years to reflect this trend. Remember when dogs were named Rover, Spot, or Bowser?

Some popular male names today are:

Sam	Gus
Buster	Sid
Jake	Travis
Blue	Jordan
Duke	Logan
Max	Bubba
Jack	Pete
Harley	Rex
Joel	Paul
Oliver	Luke
Brad	Larry
Shadow	Bailey
Toby	Reed
Rocky	Jimmy
Murphy	Charlie
Cash	Andrew
Cody	Rocky
Scruffy	Tony
Buddy	Larry

Some popular female dog names today are:

Chloe	Lucy
Sandy	Abby
Christi	Sky
Angel	Casey
Princess	Molly
Sophie	Peggy
Patty	Shannon
Lady	Lily
Debbie	Lulu
Missy	Sally
Bailey	Donna
Precious	Pam
Brandy	Connie
Misty	Maggie
Bella	Tammy
Daisy	

PET TRUSTS

Thirty nine states, including Washington, DC, have adopted laws for pet trusts. However, the laws of states have viewed that animals are property and property cannot be left property. Therefore, individuals must make a will and leave the money in a trust in the care of a guardian in order to care for their pet after their death.

Some dog benefactors receiving pet trusts are:

Flossie, a Labrador, saved Drew Barrymore's life from a house fire. Ms. Barrymore later deeded her 3,600 square foot home to her dog, Flossie.

Gunther III and Gunther IV, both German Shepherds, were willed $124 million by their master, Countess Liebenstein.

Tina and Kate, both Collie mixes, were left $450,000 each.

Trouble, a Yorkie, was left $12 million by the heiress Leona Helmsley. Her will included orders that the dog had to be walked by dog walkers daily and be served gourmet meals.

PUPPY BEHAVIOR

A new puppy can be exciting and fun but also very frustrating at times. A dog's behavior and actions are inbred, so we need to learn the behavior of that particular breed to figure them out.

As puppies are usually still teething when you bring them home, you need to be prepared. Prevention is the key, as their need to chew is unavoidable. Have chew toys for him so he will not chew your shoes or worst yet, the electrical cords in your home.

You can freeze a baby teething ring which will feel good on his gums. If your puppy is chewing on something, say NO and give him his chew toy. He will begin to understand that his toys are the only things to only chew on. If you keep him crated, be sure that there are chew toys with him inside the crate.

MOVIES FEATURING DOGS

Following is partial list of movies that have dogs in them. Some are old and some are fairly new to the box office. How many have you seen?

Snow Dogs

Fox and the Hound

Cats and Dogs

Huckleberry Hound

The Simple Life

Atomic Dog

101 & 102 Dalmatians

Mad Dogs

Lassie

Walk Like A Man

The Adventures of Rin Tin Tin

K-911

Lethal Weapon

Dog Gone Love

Wizard of Oz

Babe

Incredible Journey

Good Boy

Beethoven

Millionaire Dog

Lady and the Tramp

Fangs of the Arctic

2 Stupid Dogs

The 10th Kingdom

All Dogs Go To Heaven

Must Love Dogs

Benji

Turner & Hooch

Scooby-Doo

Air Bud

An All Dogs Christmas Carol

My Life as a Dog

White Fang

White Dog

Legally Blonde I & II

Longstreet

Amos & Andrew

Best in Show

Old Yeller

Big Red

The Shaggy Dog

Shiloh

Accidental Tourist

FAMOUS NOVELS FEATURING DOGS

Peter Pan – A Newfoundland named Nana.

The Silence of the Lambs – A Toy Poodle named Precious.

The Wizard of Oz – A Cairn Terrier named Toto.

Oliver Twist – A Staffordshire Bull Terrier named Bullseye.

The Incredible Journey – A Bull Terrier named Bodger.

Call of the Wild – A Shepherd/St. Bernard mix named Buck.

Watchers – A Golden Retriever named Einstein.

The Tale of Jemima Puddle-duck – A Collie named Kep.

Where the Red Fern Grows – A pair of Red Tick Hounds named Old Dan and Little Ann.

The Art of Racing in the Rain – A Yellow Labrador named Enzo.

Travels with Charley – A Poodle named Charley.

The Thin Man – A Schnauzer named Asta.

DOGS IN MYTHOLOGY

In ancient Egypt, cats were held in very high esteem, more so than dogs were. Inside the tombs, there are thousands of mummified cats but mummified dogs were very rare.

Here are some dogs that are mentioned in Mythology:

Anubis was the Dog-Headed God of the Dead. The Egyptians used herbs to preserve the dead. Anubis would smell the dead and determine if they smelled pure. If they did, he would then allow them to enter into the Kingdom of the Dead.

Sirius is known as the Dog Star because it appears in the constellation Canis Major or Big Dog. When Sirius would rise at sunrise, the ancient Romans thought it added heat to the sun, so Sirius meant scorching. They also referred to those days of intense heat as the Dog Days, thus our saying today of the "dog days of summer."

Maera was a hound owned by the winemaker, Icarius. When Icarius was out in the field, he was killed and buried by the shepherds. His daughter, Erigone, was worried when her father did not return, so she took Maera with her to search for her father. The dog found the grave where Icarius had been buried, and Erigone became so distraught over the killing of her father that she hung herself. The dog, Maera, was also so distraught over losing his master that he jumped off a cliff.

Argos was the dog in Homer's "Odyssey," who belonged to Odysseus. Odysseus had to fight in the Trojan War and had to leave his dog, Argos behind. There was no one to care for the dog so he wound up abandoned and lived on the streets. Odysseus had to disguise himself when he returned from the Trojan War, in order not to be killed. He saw Argos on the sidewalk and the dog was near death from starvation. Argos raised his frail head and was able to wag his tail slightly seeing the master that he had waited so long to see. Odysseus could not acknowledge him, as he was afraid he would be noticed. He had to turn and walk away from his faithful dog, but he had a tear in his eye and his heart was full of grief.

Cerberus was the hound from Greek mythology with many heads. His role was to guard the gates of Hell and not to allow any of the dead to exit through the gates.

Hecuba, the Queen of Troy, was said through the legends to have turned into a dog from the grief she felt over the deaths of her children, Polyxena and Polydorus. It is said that she became so insane from the grief over her deceased children that she started barking like a dog and eventually turned into one.

DOGS THAT HAVE APPEARED IN COMMERCIALS

Start noticing the commercials on television and the dogs that appear in them. The drug commercials, in particular, use dogs very often. Sometimes, they are directly in the commercial with the actors and sometimes they are just in the background.

Clothing manufactures also use dogs quite frequently in their ads. The models will be holding them or they will be standing by them.

Dogs conjure up a hominess and trust when we see them in commercials and advertising. Maybe this is why they are used so often.

Some famous dogs that have appeared in commercials are:

Duke - From the Bush Bean Company.

Tige - From the Buster Brown Shoe Company.

Gidget - The Taco Bell Chihuahua.

Nipper - The RCA dog.

Spuds - The Bud Light dog.

Alex - The Stroh's beer Golden Retriever.

Big Mo - The Alpo Mascot.

COMIC STRIPS THAT FEATURE DOGS

Dogs have been featured in the comic strips of newspapers for a long time, with some dating back as far as the 1950s. Some of these comic dogs are:

"Dilbert" (the dog was Dogbert)

"For Better or For Worse" (the dogs were Edgar and Farley)

"Peanuts" (the dog was Snoopy)

"Cathy" (the dogs were Vivian and Electra)

"Beetle Bailey" (the dog was Otto)

."Marmaduke" (the dog was Marmaduke)

"Cathy" (the dog was Vivian)

"Garfield" (the dog was Odie)

"Hagar the Horrible" (the dog was Snert)

"Family Circus" (the dog was Sam)

"Dennis the Menace" (the dog was Ruff)

"Fred Bassett" (the dog was Fred)

"Ziggy" (the dog was Fuzz)

"Mother Goose and Grimm" (the dog was Grimm)

SPACE DOGS

During the late 1950s and through the middle 1960s, the Soviet Union sent dogs up into space before sending man during their space program and exploration.

The following dogs have become very famous due to their space journeys:

Sputnik 2 launched into space in 1957, with Laika, a mongrel, on board. The United States nicknamed her Muttnik. Laika died during the space ordeal.

Sputnik 5 launched into space in 1960, with Belka and Strelka on board. These were the first dogs to survive the space orbit flights.

Sputnik 10 launched into space in 1961, with Zvezdochka on board. This was the final test flight with dogs before Yuri Gagarin became the first man to enter into space.

Sputnik 9 launched into space in 1961, with Chernushka on board. Chernushka was accompanied by a wooden mannequin and a few other animals.

And last but not least, were Albina and Tsyganka. They didn't actually go into space, but they were launched up to the end of the Earth's atmosphere, some 53 miles up. This was to test the spacesuits for pressure before sending a man into space. They were ejected out of their seats and returned safely to earth.

PRESIDENTS AND THEIR DOGS

All sorts of gifts were given to Presidents in office. These gifts included animals of all sorts but the gifts were mainly dogs.

One of the most famous gifts was the dog given to President Kennedy by Soviet Premier Nikita Khrushchev named Pushinka, which means "Fluffy" in Russian. The Premier wanted the gift to be a symbol of the reduced Cold War Tension between the Soviet Union and the United States. The dog was immediately turned over to the CIA and was sent to the Walter Reed Hospital. The dog was x-rayed for possible transmitting devices that could be hidden under his skin. When none were found, the dog was returned to the White House and the Kennedy family. Pushinka was the daughter of Strelka, who rode in Sputnik 5.

Calvin Coolidge had a Wire Fox Terrier named Peter Pan. To say the least, Peter Pan was quite wild and was excited when visitors came to the White House. One day a woman visiting the White House had on a full skirt made of a very light material. Peter Pan leaped onto her skirt and tore it off the woman. A White House aide removed his suit jacket and quickly placed it around the woman's waist. After this incident, President Coolidge's wife sent Peter Pan back to their home in Massachusetts but kept the Collies that were hers in the White House.

Terriers have been the most popular dog breeds owned by U.S. presidents. Some of the presidents that owned terriers were John F. Kennedy, Herbert Hoover, George W. Bush, Richard Nixon, Franklin D. Roosevelt, Woodrow Wilson, James Buchanan and Theodore Roosevelt. The terriers they owned were the Scottish Terriers, Rat Terriers, Bull Terriers, Manchester Terriers, Toy Terriers, Fox Terriers, Yorkshire Terriers and Welsh Terriers. The Scottish terriers were the most common.

Franklin D. Roosevelt's dog was a Scottish Terrier named Fala. FDR took him everywhere and Fala even slept with him. FDR died when Fala was only five years old. His wife, Eleanor, stated that the dog never stopped looking and waiting for his master until his death at age 12.

President James Garfield named his dog Veto.

Lyndon B. Johnson named his beagles Him and Her. LBJ was photographed at the White House picking up one of the beagles by its ears. This caused a tremendous outcry by the public.

George Bush said that his dog Millie would shower with him every morning in the White House.

It is said that Harry Truman did not care too much for dogs. The Irish Setter that was in the White House did not stay too long.

The dog that Richard Nixon was most fond of was an Irish Setter named King Timahoe, not the Cocker Spaniel named Checkers that was the most popular in the news.

Dwight D. Eisenhower liked Scottish Terriers. He had two, one was named Telek, and the other was named Caaci.

The dog that was John F. Kennedy's favorite was a Welsh Terrier named Charlie. He had owned Charlie prior to his inauguration into the White House as President.

PRESIDENTS AND THE BREEDS THEY OWNED

Bill Clinton – Labrador

George Washington – Hound

Richard Nixon – Irish Setter

Gerald Ford – Golden Retriever

George W. Bush – Scottish Terrier

Calvin Coolidge – Collie

Herbert Hoover – Fox Terrier

Dwight D. Eisenhower – Weimaraner

George Bush – Springer Spaniel

Ulysses S. Grant – Newfoundland

Ronald Reagan – Cavalier King Charles Spaniel

OFFICIAL STATE DOGS

There are eight states that have designated dogs as their official state dog. Listed below are the states, the dog breed and the year of the designation. Notice that the states listed are mainly on the east coast.

Texas	Blue Lacy	2005
North Carolina	Plott Hound	1989
Wisconsin	American Water Spaniel	1985
South Carolina	Boykin Spaniel	1985
Massachusetts	Boston Terrier	1979
Louisiana	Catahoula Leopard Dog	1979
Virginia	American Foxhound	1966
Pennsylvania	Great Dane	1965
Maryland	Chesapeake Bay Retriever	1964

INTERESTING DOG TALES OF FAMOUS CELEBRITIES

Elvis Presley really loved Bloodhounds. This may be the reason for his hit song "You Ain't Nothin' But A Hound Dog." He also owned a Maltese named "Foxhugh."

While visiting in England, Elizabeth Taylor and her husband, the late Richard Burton, lived on their boat on the Thames with their Pekingese and Lhasa Apso. They did this in order to avoid the six month quarantine that is required for dogs to enter into the country.

The tough characters that Humphrey Bogart portrayed in his movie roles were carried over into his love for Boxers and Scottish Terriers, who are also considered tough characters in the dog world.

FAMOUS PEOPLE AND THEIR DOGS

Afghan Hound	Bernese Mountain Dog
Pablo Picasso	Robert Redford
Airedale	Bichon Frisé
John Wayne	Barbara Streisand
	Betty White
Akita	Frank Gifford
Cher	James Arness
Dan Aykroyd	Tanya Tucker
Helen Keller	
	Bloodhound
Alaskan Malamute	Charles Dickens
Cheryl Ladd	
Dom DeLuise	Border Collie
	Sarah Jessica Parker
Basset Hound	
Arthur Miller	Borzoi
James Earl Jones	Nick Nolte
Marilyn Monroe	
	Boston Terrier
Beagle	Vincent Price
Eva Gabor	Yves St. Laurent
Bearded Collie	
Bo Derek	
Boxer	Red Buttons
Alan Ladd	

Andy Williams	**Chow Chow**
Charlton Heston	Kelsey Grammer
Douglas Fairbanks, Jr.	Martha Stewart
Humphrey Bogart	Ringo Starr
Jodie Foster	Sigmund Freud
Nat King Cole	Uma Thurman
Robin Williams	Walt Disney
Steffi Graf	
	Cocker Spaniel
Bull Terrier	Charlize Theron
Fred Estaire	Ernest Hemingway
George Patton	Fred McMurray
John Steinbeck	Lauren Bacall
	Liberace
Bulldog	Oprah Winfrey
Olivia De Havilland	Phyllis Diller
Truman Capote	Tom Selleck
Cairn Terrier	**Collie**
David Hasselhoff	Art Linkletter
	Doris Day
Cavalier King Charles Spaniel	J.P. Morgan
Duke of Marlborough	Judy Garland
Frank Sinatra	Marilyn Monroe
Kirk Douglas	Paul Newman
Mary Heart	Randolph Scott
Michael J. Fox	Walter Mondale
Chihuahua	**Corgi**
Hilary Duff	Mickey Rooney
Paula Abdul	
Dachshund	Zsa Zsa Gabor
Clark Gable	

Patty Duke	**Golden Retriever**
Rita Hayworth	Arnold Palmer
Winona Judd	Bill Blass
	Gregory Peck
Dalmatian	James Stewart
Eugene O'Neil	Jamie Lee Curtis
Jane Alexander	Jane Seymour
Michael J. Fox	Jimmy Buffet
Richard Simmons	Kim Novak
	Mary Tyler Moore
Doberman Pinscher	Matt Lauer
Raquel Welch	Neil Diamond
	Norman Vincent Peale
English Sheepdog	Pamela Anderson
Paul McCartney	Renee Zellweger
	Ron Howard
Fox Terrier	
Agatha Christie	**Great Dane**
Cheryl Tiegs	James Brolin
Lucille Ball	Jim Carey
Martina Navratilova	William Shatner
Maureen O'Sullivan	Wilt Chamberlain
German Shepherd	**Greyhound**
Debra Winger	Prince Albert
Elton John	Sigourney Weaver
Jacqueline Kennedy	
Robert Schuller	**Irish Setter**
Roy Rogers	Brigitte Bardot
Steffi Graf	Jimmy Durante
Stephanie Powers	
Italian Greyhound	**Henry David Thoreau**
Peter the Great	

	Mastiff
Jack Russell Terrier	Alexander the Great
Prince Charles	Douglas Fairbanks
Wynonna Judd	Kirstie Alley
	Marlin Brando
Kerry Blue Terrier	Sylvester Stallone
John Huston	
	Miniature Schnauzer
Labrador Retriever	Robert Dole
Sarah McLachlan	
Barbara Mandrell	**Newfoundland**
Gary Collins	Sally Struthers
George McGovern	
Harrison Ford	**Norwich Terrier**
Henry Kissinger	Lily Tomlin
Kevin Costner	Oscar de la Renta
Meg Ryan	
Prince Charles	**Old English Sheepdog**
Princess Anne	Charles Osgood
Sheryl Crow	Jean Harlow
Sylvester Stallone	Katherine Ross
Tom Cruise	
Steve Martin	**Pekingese**
	Shirley Temple
Lhasa Apso	
Burt Bacharach	**Pomeranian**
	Isaac Newton
Maltese	Kate Hudson
Elizabeth Taylor	LeAnn Rimes
Elvis Presley	Michelangelo
Halle Berry	Tammy Wynette
Poodle	**Schnauzer**
Barbara Eden	Bruce Lee

Cary Grant	Heloise
Debbie Reynolds	Steve McQueen
Don Rickles	Sugar Ray Leonard
Elke Sommer	
Gypsy Rose Lee	Scottish Terrier
Jack Lemmon	Bette Davis
Jaclyn Smith	Marlo Thomas
James Thurber	
Mary Kay Ash	Shih Tzu
Tallulah Bankhead	Mariah Carey
Winston Churchill	Phyllis Diller
Pug	**Siberian Husky**
Paula Abdul	Kate Jackson
Woody Harrelson	King Edward VII
Jessica Alba	
	Skye Terrier
Rhodesian Ridgeback	**Robert Lewis Stevenson**
Whoopi Goldberg	
	Springer Spaniel
Rottweiler	**Jayne Meadows**
Carrie Fisher	Jimmy Buffett
Curt Schilling	Mel Torme
Elvira	Steve Allen
Sally Jessie Raphael	
Sid Caesar	Toy Poodle
Will Smith	Ivana Trump
Samoyed	**West Highland White Terrier**
James Garner	Charles Darwin
Patrick Wayne	Joan Fontaine
Yorkshire Terrier	
Audrey Hepburn	

Demi Moore	
Joan Rivers	
Joe Garagiola	
Justin Timberlake	
Kirsten Dunst	

BULLDOGS THAT WERE USED AS MASCOTS

The oldest college mascot was a Bulldog named Handsome Dan. In 1892, the Bulldog was chosen by Yale University as the first "live" mascot.

The University of Georgia also chose a Bulldog for the courage and tenaciousness that the breed conjures up to represent their university. They named it Uga, taken from their name the U of GA. Sports Illustrated named Uga the number one U.S. mascot; he appeared on the magazine cover of Sports Illustrated on three different issues.

The U.S. Marine Corps also chose as their mascot a Bulldog named Jiggs. The dog died before turning five years old. Since the death of Jiggs, the Marines have had succeeding Bulldog mascots and all have been named Chesty.

GO DOGGIE GREEN

Earth Day is April 22, and pet owners are buying more environmentally friendly products for their pets today. Pet manufacturers are offering more "green" pet products for the conscious-minded consumer.

Here are some tips to Doggie-Green your pet:

ひ Training pads are now available with 100% biodegradable materials.

ひ Use all-natural stain and odor removers for your carpet and clothing in place of harsh household cleaners.

ひ Grooming supplies, such as combs and brushes, are being made of recycled rubber.

ひ Use pet shampoos and conditioners with 100% natural ingredients.

ひ If you live in snow country, do not use rock salt that is sold for melting the snow and ice. The salt can contaminate the standing water.

ひ Adopt from a rescue group or local animal shelter.

ひ Scoop your poop up with biodegradable poop bags. The manufacturing of these bags uses less gas emissions, as the bags are made from an agricultural origin. If left on the ground, the rain can wash the poop into the streets.

ひ Buy dog collars and leashes made of hemp or organic cotton which are grown without pesticides and dyes. They also have collars and leashes made from recycled polyester that are made from water bottles and other plastic items. This certainly helps to keep these products out of our over-crowded landfills.

❧ Spay or neuter your pet.

❧ Use natural fertilizers on your lawn and garden.

❧ Buy dog toys made from recycled materials instead of the hard plastic that many are made from. Better yet, make your own toys out of socks or old tee shirts. Just tie a knot in them and play catch with your dog. Do not give panty hose as they could swallow those.

❧ There are dog waste composters on the market today.

❧ Buy organic fruits and vegetables from your local farmers market. If you buy locally, you are also saving on the fuel costs the supplier has for their local deliveries.

❧ Last but not least, homemade dog food is great for the environment, as there are no cans or bags to dispose of.

ASTROLOGY SIGNS

Astrology is one of the ancient sciences that were created by the ancient Egyptians. They divided the sky into 12 segments, and the Zodiac signs were named after the constellations that are in each of these twelve segments.

Astrology signs can play an important part in our human lives, as well as our pets. Mood swings and bad behavior may be due to the positioning of the stars and planets. The Zodiac signs and their meanings derive from the day, month and time of birth of that person (or dog in this case.) There are certain characteristics and traits that are symbolic with each sign of the Zodiac. If you know your dog's birthday, have fun reading about them.

See if your dog's astrological sign is compatible with your astrological sign.

AQUARIUS: January 20–February 18

Aquarius, the Water-Bearer: Compatible with Libra, Gemini, Aquarius, and Pisces.

Devoted to family, but they are also very friendly to strangers. They love freedom and are not comfortable with daily routine. They love other dogs and cats, so this is not a good choice for a one dog family because they need that companionship. They are very verbal and don't like a lot of petting.

PISCES: February 19–March 19

Pisces, the Fish: Compatible with Aquarius, Cancer, and Scorpio.

This dog is very kind and sensitive. They can communicate with their masters and feel their feelings and moods. They are easily excitable, so speak softly to them to help soothe their feelings. They tend to be a protector, and they try to make things right in the home if there is an upset. Likes routine and loves water. They just may jump in the pool with you.

ARIES: March 20–April 18

Aries, the Ram: Compatible with Leo, Gemini, Scorpio, and Libra.

This dog is always active and looking for adventure. They are very loyal to their owner and make a good companion. Likes a variety of games and loves to play rough, because they always want to win. Keep them occupied with lots of toys to play with. The Aries dog will be the leader of the pack if you have more than one pet.

TAURUS: April 19–May 20

Taurus, the Bull: Compatible with Scorpio, Capricorn, and Libra.

Loves to be pampered and loves good food. They are very content sitting for hours and this is where they get the definition of being a lazy dog. They love children and will protect them and their owners if they think they are being threatened. They are possessive of what they consider their toys, which includes also their owner. Watch the diet as they get older, as they tend to put on weight.

GEMINI: May 21–June 20

Gemini, the Twins: Compatible with Libra, Virgo, and Sagittarius.

Very independent and likes lots of attention. These dogs are very energetic and like to bark at people and objects. They can almost show too much independence, and will come to you when they want to be petted and pampered and not before. They love to run around the house, or the yard, and chase their tails or to chase absolutely nothing.

CANCER: June 21–July 22

Cancer, the Crab: Compatible with Scorpio, Pisces, and Aquarius.

What a homebody! They are a great protector to their owner and the children who live in the household. They love children and also their own toys. Give them a lot of toys because they like to collect them. They are not too much of a traveler and would rather stay home. They tend to follow you from room to room because they always want to be near their owner.

LEO: July 23–August 22

Leo, the Lion: Compatible with Scorpio, Leo, and Capricorn.

Absolutely loves to have attention and to be admired. They are the leader dogs, and they make excellent show animals. They love to have house guests, and they also enjoy being with other dogs or cats. They love the sun, so make a place where they can sit in it during the day. Give them lots of love and attention because they hate to be ignored and not talked to.

VIRGO: August 23–September 22

Virgo, the Virgin: Compatible with Taurus, Aquarius, and Gemini.

Routine is so much a part of their lives to the point of it being almost funny. They love to eat at the same time of day, wake up at the same time, and go to bed at the same time. They tend to be a one person dog, but they do like the company of another dog or cat in the household. They are easily trained, probably because they like the routine of it.

LIBRA: September 23–October 22

Libra, the Scales: Compatible with Aries, Aquarius, and Taurus.

This dog can be very persuasive, but yet gentle and affectionate. They tend to be lazy and change their minds a lot about what they want. This is an air sign, so don't give them too much smothering or petting until they want it from you. They are very charming, but they like things their own way.

SCORPIO: October 23–November 21

Scorpio, the Scorpion: Compatible with Capricorn, Pisces, and Leo.

This dog has very strong likes and dislikes. It is either very important to them, or they ignore it, and you. They like calmness since they are a water sign, but yet they are easily excitable. They can also be very stubborn when it comes to training them. They are a born leader and have an exceptional memory of things and people.

SAGITTARIUS: November 22–December 21

Sagittarius, the Archer: Compatible with Virgo, Gemini, Taurus, and Aries.

They are wanderers and love to travel. They want to be outside in the yard. They want and they demand attention, but also they like to spend some time alone. They love to learn new tricks and to be active, but they can also be very lazy when they want to be. They hate to be tied down, so give them lots of exercise.

CAPRICORN: December 22–January 19

Capricorn, the Goat: Compatible with Gemini, Virgo, Aries, and Taurus.

They are the earth sign, so if you have this dog he may want to dig holes in your yard so that he can connect with the earth. They also love routine in the household. They may tend to be moody if you try something new that they are not familiar with. They are a good judge of character, so be aware if your dog does not like the stranger.

BIRTHSTONES

The history of birthstones has been used for centuries to give luck to the person who wears them. Each month has a stone dedicated to that particular month.

It might be fun to have a collar made special with your dog's birthstone on it.

Note that the birthstones can overlap the months of the Zodiac signs. Here is the list of Birthstones according to each month:

JANUARY:

Birthstone: Garnet: Looks like a dark ruby, but less expensive.

FEBRUARY:

Birthstone: Amethyst: Purple gemstone.

MARCH:

Birthstone: Bloodstone: Light green or blue earth stones.

APRIL:

Birthstone: Diamond: Durable and represents purity.

MAY:

Birthstone: Emerald: Green stone and used for energy healing.

JUNE:

Birthstone: Alexandrite: The modern birthstone for this month is the Pearl. Pearls are symbols for love.

JULY:

Birthstone: Ruby: Deep red color and this stone is known for love.

AUGUST:

Birthstone: Sardonyx: Small black stones.

SEPTEMBER:

Birthstone: Sapphire: Comes in all colors except red. Blue is the most common color.

OCTOBER:

Birthstone: Tourmaline: Most common colors are pink and green.

NOVEMBER:

Birthstone: Citrine: Beautiful shades of yellow.

DECEMBER:

Birthstone: Turquoise: Vibrant light blue stones.

SOME COMMON DOG SAYINGS

To err is human, to forgive, canine.

When you feel "dog-tired" at night, maybe it's because you growled all day.

"Barking up the wrong tree."

"In a perfect world, every dog would have a home and every home would have a dog."

"A spoiled rotten dog lives here."

"Let sleeping dogs lie."

"The tail wagging the dog."

"Wipe your paws."

"I love dogs."

"When please doesn't work, beg."

"If you want the best seat in the house, move the dog."

"My dog's not spoiled...I'm just well trained."

"Be tuff...the "dog days" of summer can be wuff."

"Dogs are people too."

"A house is not a home without a dog."

"Husband and dog missing...reward for dog."

"A boy's best friend is his dog."

"Recycle bones here."

"Chasing your tail gets you nowhere…except back to where you started."

"As sick as a dog."

"Hot Dog!"

"Top Dog."

"Dog tired."

"Dog eat dog."

"Raining like cats and dogs."

"Work like a dog."

"You can't teach an old dog new tricks."

"Put on the dog."

"Every dog has its day."

Dog Section IV

BREED BEHAVIOR

Choose the breed of dog that best serves your lifestyle.

If your dog has a constant behavior problem after months of trying to train him, he may not be able to help it.

Dogs were bred to do specific jobs, according to their breed. An example is that if you have a terrier that barks and chases cats or squirrels around, it is because it is the breed of the dog. They were designed to hunt and furrow for rabbits, rats and squirrels. The Romans named them "terrarii" after the Latin word for earth.

There are six different groups of dogs that are classified under breeds. These breeds are:

THE HOUND GROUP

THE SPORTING GROUP

THE TERRIER GROUP

THE NON-SPORTING GROUP

THE WORKING GROUP

THE TOY GROUP

Choosing a breed of dog to fit your lifestyle requires some homework on your part. Dog breeds have certain characteristics particular to them. It is very hard to "re-train" a dog if that is how they were bred. Your dog's dependence on its master never ends, so it is very important to be able to fulfill that obligation to them. The dog depends on its master for all of its love, nourishment, medical needs, grooming and exercise. You owe it to your dog to choose one that fits both your lifestyles.

BREED TIDBITS

Studies have found that the HOUND BREEDS were some of the oldest breeds of dogs, with some dating back to 3,000 to 5,000 B.C.

SOME OF THESE ANCIENT BREEDS OF DOGS INCLUDE THE FOLLOWING:

Saluki

Siberian Husky

Afghan hound

Greyhound

Chow Chow

Pekingese

Lhasa Apso

Samoyed

Akita

Shih Tzu

Alaskan Malamute

Shar Pei

Tibetan Terrier

SMALL AND LARGE BREEDS

People are fascinated by the small dog breeds. They can make ideal "child substitutes", while bigger dog breeds make good companion dogs. Small dogs are easy to pick up and cuddle like a child, and can give the owner almost a parental feeling for them.

This inborn parental feeling that humans have for their small dog makes them become very protective of them and very emotionally attached. Many small dog owners refer to their dog as their "baby."

SOME OF THE SMALLEST DOG BREEDS INCLUDE THE FOLLOWING:

Chihuahua   Maltese
Yorkshire Terrier   Papillion

SOME OF THE LARGEST DOG BREEDS INCLUDE THE FOLLOWING:

Great Dane   English Mastiff
Irish wolfhound   Borzoi
St. Bernard   Turkish Shepherd

HOUND GROUP

They can hunt people, animals, and birds, but they do not kill their hunted prey. You will need an enclosed yard because they may want to escape and go hunting for their prey. As a general rule, they make excellent house pets, but they do need to be exercised daily. They tend to sometimes not bark, but bay. If you have ever heard a dog bay, it is quite interesting. This group is some of the earliest recorded in history, and they were used exclusively for hunting. They can hunt by either sight or smell, as their sense of smell is very acute. A few in this category are:

Basset hound	Greyhound
Bloodhound	Afghan hound
Whippet	Saluki
English foxhound	Basenji
Irish wolfhound	Foxhound
Dachshund	Borzoi
Beagle	Rhodesian Ridgeback

SPORTING GROUP

These dogs are smart and energetic and were developed to hunt like the Hound Group, but were used primarily for game hunting. This group includes the Spaniels, Pointers, Setters, and Retrievers.

They all have well-developed noses for smelling, as well as long ears to protect them when they run into the woods to retrieve the game. The Retrievers, being excellent swimmers, were used to hunt waterfowl. They would jump into the water to retrieve the birds that the hunter had shot down.

The Pointers would flush the birds out of the bushes or they would just "point" to the birds for the hunter to see. All the dogs in this Sporting Group make wonderful family dogs. A few in this category are:

Cocker Spaniel

Labrador Retriever

Irish Setter

Weimaraner

Pointer

Brittany Spaniel

English Setter

Golden Retriever

English Springer Spaniel

Chesapeake By Retriever

German Short-Haired Pointer

Basset Griffon Vendeen

Vizsla

Bracco Italiano

English Cocker Spaniel

TERRIER GROUP

This group was specifically bred to hunt for rats, fox, and rabbits. They were also used in many of the wars because they were very rugged and enduring.

Their body tends to be short-legged in most of the breeds, although the Airedale tends to have a larger leg size. Their coats can be smooth with shorter hair or long with coarser hair.

They can be very energetic and also be very temperamental. They are quick to learn and very loyal to their master. They make a wonderful house pet or apartment pet, but they do require lots of exercise and training. A few in this category are:

Airedale Terrier

Manchester Terrier

Cairn Terrier

Bull Terrier

Wire Fox Terrier

Norfolk Terrier

Miniature Schnauzer

Giant Schnauzer

Welsh Terrier

Smooth Fox Terrier

Scottish Terrier

Dandie Dinmont Terrier

Jack Russell Terrier

West Highland White Terrier

Australian Terrier

Soft-Coated Wheaten Terrier

Irish Terrier

Norwich Terrier

Bedlington Terrier

Sealyham Terrier

American Staffordshire Terrier

Staffordshire Bull Terrier

Skye Terrier

Border Terrier

Kerry Blue Terrier

NON-SPORTING GROUP

This group is a most interesting breed, and has the largest distinctive group of all the other breeds. These dogs were bred centuries ago to perform specific functions, and they have a certain look appeal. They come in a variety of different sizes and shapes from small to fairly large.

They are very easy to train, which makes them excellent competitors in dog shows. They are also used extensively as circus dogs. They are very easy-going and make great companion dogs for home or apartment dwellers. They also serve as excellent watchdogs over their master and home. A few in this category are:

Bichon Frisé

Chow Chow

Lhasa Apso

Tibetan Spaniel

Boston Terrier

Shar Pei

Poodles

Keeshond

Dalmatian

Schipperke

Bulldog

WORKING AND HERDING GROUP

Around twenty thousand years ago or so, man used the fur of this breed for shelter and warmth, and possibly even for his food. They also used this breed of dog for a variety of tasks. They helped them hunt for small animals and fowl, served as watchdogs with their keen sense of smell and hearing, and they herded their sheep and cattle.

This breed is also known as the police, rescue, sight-seeing, and hearing dogs. Their main instinct is to guard their master and property. They need lots of exercise to be a house dog and they become very affectionate and loyal to their owner. A few in this category are:

Boxer

Mastiff

Great Dane

Newfoundland

Doberman Pinscher

Old English Sheepdog

Siberian Husky

Great Pyrenees

St. Bernard

Shetland Sheepdog

Akita

Welsh Corgi

Bullmastiff

German Shepherd

Rottweiler

Alaskan Malamute

Samoyed

Australian Cattledog

Standard Schnauzer

Belgian Sheepdog

Border Collie

Bouvier Des Flandres

Bearded Collie

Burmese Mountain Dog

Rough-Coated Collie

MIXED BREEDS

Cross Breed vs. Mixed Breed:

If you acquire a "cross breed" dog, it means that there were only two different breeds of dogs that were combined.

If you acquire a "mixed breed" dog, it means that there could have been numerous breeds of dogs that were combined. Mixed breeds tend to be healthier, as they do not suffer from the diseases and disabilities that "pure-bred" dogs tend to have.

Mixed breeds are not recognized by the American Kennel Club, but mixed breeds have become more popular in the recent years. In fact, they are becoming known as "Designer Dogs", and some are even more expensive to buy than the Purebreds.

Here are some mixed breeds that are becoming quite popular:

Goldenpoodles (Golden Retriever and Poodle)

Puggles (Pug and Beagle)

Labradoodles (Labrador and Poodle)

Schnoodles (Miniature Schnauzer and Poodle)

Terripoos (Terrier and Poodle)

Peke-a-Poos (Pekingese and Poodle)

Puggle (Pug and Beagle)

Cock-a-Chon (Cocker Spaniel and Bichon Frisé)

Silkese (Silky Terrier and Maltese)

Yorkinese (Yorkshire Terrier and Pekingese)

Bea-Tzu (Beagle and Shih Tzu)

Posies (Pomeranian and Shetland Sheepdog)

Snorkie (Miniature Schnauzer and Yorkshire Terrier)

Maltapoo (Maltese and Poodle)

Cockapoo (Cocker Spaniel and Poodle)

MONGRELS

The Mongrel is not a breed at all. It is a dog of mixed and unknown breeds and can have various interbreeding as well. The mongrel is also known as the "mutt", and it is usually very healthy because of its survival.

They tend to be less disease prone and are usually even tempered. They come in all sizes and shapes and make adorable and loving companions. This type of dog is usually the one found at the animal shelters or at the Humane Society. Be sure and look at these places if you are in the market for a dog, or maybe a companion for the one you already have.

In addition to the breed divisions, dogs are also classified into different categories. Here are a few examples:

AFFECTIONATE AND FRIENDLY

Bichon Frisé

Collie

Cocker Spaniel

Labrador Retriever

Golden Retriever

Keeshond

Old English Sheepdog

Cavalier King Charles Spaniel

English Setter

DOMINANT AND PROTECTIVE

Bull Terrier

Weimaraner

Akita

Rottweiler

Boxer

Schnauzer

Chow Chow

Puli

Bullmastiff

TRAINABLE AND CLEVER DOGS

German Shepherd

Doberman Pinscher

Border Collie

Poodle

Poodle

Papillon

GOOD NATURED

Bulldog

Bloodhound

St. Bernard

Basset Hound

Great Dane

Mastiff

Beagle

Newfoundland

HOME LOVING DOGS

Pug

Whippet

Maltese

Dachshund

Lhasa Apso

Chihuahua

Boston Terrier

Pomeranian

Pekingese

Greyhound

INDEPENDENT AND PERSONABLE

Dalmatian

Pointer

Saluki

Afghan Hound

Samoyed

Irish Setter

Siberian Husky

Shar Pei

Borzoi

DOG CARE

Dogs are such an important part of our lives, but they depend solely on us for their total care and needs. They are truly members of our families Dog services have sprung up in recent years to accommodate and pamper our pets.

Some of these services include:

24 Hour Emergency Clinics, Doggie Day Care Centers, Dog Spas, Dental Products, Organic Foods, Holistic Veterinarians, Vitamin and Mineral Products, Doggie Parks, Mobile Groomers, Dog Strollers, Fashion Beds, Mobile Veterinarians, Organic Leashes and Collars, Organic Bedding, Fashion Clothing, and Dog Bakeries.

DENTAL HEALTH

Dental health is an important part in pet care. Here is some information on dental care for your dog.

Warning Signs of Periodontal (Gum) Disease:

Bad breath
Yellowish crust near the gum
Difficulty eating
Loose or missing teeth
Red or swollen gums
No signs at all, but still may have the beginnings of the disease

Periodontal (gum) disease is a very common health problem in dogs. Plaque build-up and bacteria can infect the gum tissue, resulting in tooth loss. The bacteria can also enter the blood stream through the blood vessels near the gums and teeth, and can affect the lungs, heart, other organs, and even the brain.

If you start brushing your dog's teeth when it is a puppy, they will be used to it. For an older dog, they may resist, but they will get accustomed to it if you keep trying. Regular brushing will help prevent this dental disease.

Do not use human toothpaste because it may be toxic to your dog. Also, human toothbrushes are too big for your dog's mouth. You need to buy pet toothpaste and toothbrushes for your dog.

To get your dog used to brushing, have him taste the toothpaste for a couple days. After that, use your finger with the toothpaste on it, and act like you are brushing. You can wear rubber gloves if you prefer. After a few days of this, put the toothpaste on a brush and start to brush the teeth. If he gets fussy, stop immediately so you don't scare him. After he settles down, you can then revert back to your finger with the toothpaste on it.

If you are uncomfortable brushing your dog's teeth, your veterinarian can perform this for you. Anesthesia-free dental cleaning is now available through a network of veterinarians. Check with your veterinarian to see if they have this cleaning available in their office.

Dental care is such an important factor in the health of your pet.

POISONOUS PLANTS

Poisonous plants are also an important part of pet care. The following list contains some popular plants that may be poisonous or toxic to your dog:

Azalea

English Ivy

Holly Berries

Hydrangea

Iris

Laurel

Lilies

Lilies

Mistletoe Berries

Oleander

Poinsettias

Sago Palm

Yew

Here are a few dog safety tips to be aware of:

If you have children, make sure your dog cannot get to their toys. If he were to chew one, he could choke on a part that may come off in his mouth.

Watch out for electrical cords. If your dog decides to chew on it, he can get electrocuted.

Antifreeze is very deadly to dogs, and unfortunately, they like the taste. Keep the container off the floor and watch the garage floor and driveway for traces of it.

Keep all lawn chemicals and pesticides where your dog can never reach them.

Rat poison is very deadly.

Watch out for the trash can. If you put bones in it and your dog gets into the trash, he could choke on the bones. Or, in the bathroom, if you throw a bottle of medicine in the trash, he may think it is a toy because it rattles and swallow the medicine which could be toxic or even deadly.

If you drop paper clips, pens, pencils, rubber bands, or staples on the floor, pick them up before your dog does. If he swallows one of these items, he could require surgery if it gets stuck inside the throat.

Rawhide chews are digestible. However, if you give your dog rawhide chews and they chew it down to a size that can be swallowed whole, throw it out because they could choke on it. A "soggy" chew can be left to dry out and harden again, so don't throw them out if your dog walks away from it.

NEVER EVER leave your dog in a car in the summer, even for a minute. The inside temperature can reach up to 160 degrees. Even with the windows cracked, it could result in brain damage or even death. Some states are making it illegal to leave a dog in the car. It's too bad not all states are changing to that law.

Do not use the toilet cleaners that are placed inside the tank. If your pet would ever drink from the toilet, it could be poisoned by the toilet cleaner that is in the water.

Have your veterinarian's phone number and the 24-Hour Emergency Clinic phone number handy in case of an emergency. In the stress of an emergency, time is of the essence. Keep the numbers on the refrigerator or in an address book. You could save precious minutes by not having to look up the number.

Be aware if you throw sticks to your dog to fetch. They could land upwards in the ground and your racing dog could get injured.

Nicotine can be very poisonous for your dog. Keep cigarettes and other nicotine-related products (patches-gum-lozenges) out of reach.

If your dog gets bitten by a snake, do NOT cut open the site. Also, do NOT try to suck out the venom. Instead, apply ice to the bite and keep pressure on it to slow up the flow of toxins into the body. Get to the veterinarian quickly and try to keep the dog as calm as possible. If you saw the snake, try to describe it to the veterinarian to determine if it is poisonous or not.

If your dog has heatstroke, try to cool him down as quickly as possible by putting him in a bathtub of lukewarm water or drape a wet towel over him. Try to get him to drink water if he can. Dogs with shorter noses are more at risk for heatstroke. This is because dogs control their body temperature by increasing their rate of breathing, and a longer nose can take in more oxygen.

Cat Section V

CAT SECTION

There are a number of households who not only own dogs, but have a cat in the household as well.

A homemade diet for the felines in the family could prove beneficial to their health and longevity as well.

Following are some recipes that are for the cat in the family. There are treats and meals to try using a mixture of canned cat food and dry cat food, along with fresh ingredients.

CAT TREATS

BAKED TUNA BALLS

CHICKEN LIVER/GIZZARD BALLS

BEEF LIVER TREATS

SARDINE TREAT

BAKED TUNA BALLS

1 (6 ounce) can tuna in water, undrained

1/4 cup mashed potatoes, leftover or instant

1/4 cup nonfat dry milk

1 large egg, whisked

Preheat oven to 350 degrees and spray a cookie sheet. Break up the tuna with a fork and add the potatoes, dry milk, and the whisked egg. Stir until blended thoroughly. Drop by teaspoon full onto the greased cookie sheet and bake for 12 minutes or longer until slightly browned. Let cool and give as a treat. Freeze leftovers and take a few out at a time to thaw at room temperature.

🐾 Tuna goes on sale quite frequently, so watch for specials and stock up. The store brand of tuna is less expensive.

🐾🐾 If you don't want to turn the oven on, you can scramble the egg in a skillet and then add the tuna, potatoes, and dry milk all together in the skillet. Let cool and serve. Refrigerate any leftovers for up to three days.

CHICKEN LIVER /GIZZARD BALLS

3 chicken gizzards, rinsed

2 chicken livers, rinsed

1 large egg, whisked

2 tablespoons chicken broth

Place the chicken gizzards and livers in a small pan of water and boil for approximately 15 minutes until almost done. Preheat the oven to 375 degrees and grease a cookie sheet. Drain the gizzards and livers and put into a food processor. Puree until smooth. Then add the egg and the chicken broth. Drop by teaspoons onto the cookie sheet and bake until browned, about 12 minutes. Let cool and serve. Refrigerate any leftovers for up to three days.

Add a pinch of garlic powder to the water the gizzards and livers cook in for extra flavor and a better aroma while cooking.

BEEF LIVER TREATS

1 pound beef livers

1/4 teaspoon garlic powder

1 tablespoon olive oil

Put the olive oil in a skillet and fry the livers sprinkled with the garlic powder on medium heat until done. This should take about 15 minutes. Keep turning them to brown on all sides. Let cool and cut into bite size pieces with kitchen shears for a lovely treat. Refrigerate for up to three days.

🐾 Livers do tend to burn quickly, so keep them on medium to low heat. If they are starting to brown too quickly before they are done, add a little water to the skillet.

🐾🐾 Chicken livers can also be substituted.

SARDINE TREAT

1 can sardines, drained

2 tablespoons instant brown rice, cooked

Break up the sardines with a fork and mix in the cooked rice. Serve a tablespoon for a nice treat. Refrigerate any leftovers for three days.

🐾 Cook up several cups of instant brown rice to keep on hand. Refrigerate in covered container and add more water or broth if needed to reheat.

🐾🐾 This is very rich, so a tablespoon will be a nice treat.

CAT RECIPES

OATMEAL MADNESS

EGG AND TUNA SCRAMBLE

EGGS & BACON

ZUCCHINI YUM-YUM

THANKSGIVING AGAIN

CRUNCHY ROAST BEEF

LIVER & RICE

PARSLEY SALMON

BREAKFAST MEOW

OATMEAL MADNESS

1 (6 ounce) can cat food, any flavor

1/4 cup cooked instant oatmeal, regular flavor

2 tablespoons cottage cheese, small curd

1/4 cup dry cat food, pulverized

Break up the canned cat food in a bowl. Add the cooked oatmeal, cottage cheese and dry cat food. Mix well and serve. Refrigerate any leftovers for up to three days.

🐾 Cook up several cups of instant oatmeal and keep covered in the refrigerator. You will need to add more water when reheating.

🐾🐾 Process several cups of dry cat food in a food processor or blender and keep on hand. Pulverizing the cat food makes the dish easier to eat. Keep the food in a sealed container for freshness.

EGG AND TUNA SCRAMBLE

1 (6 ounce) can tuna, packed in water and drained

2 large eggs, whisked

2 tablespoons grated cheddar cheese

1/4 cup shredded zucchini, uncooked

Scramble the eggs in a skillet with a little olive oil. Turn off the burner and add the drained tuna, the grated cheese, and the zucchini. Let this cool and serve. Refrigerate any leftovers for up to three days.

🐾 This is a great way to use up eggs that have passed the expiration date on the carton. But be sure they are still good. Fill a bowl with water and if they float, throw them out. If they stay on the bottom, they are still good.

EGGS & BACON

2 bacon slices, cooked and diced

2 large eggs, whisked

1/4 cup cottage cheese, small curd

2 tablespoons shredded cheddar cheese

Cut the bacon into dice with kitchen shears or fry the slices whole and then crumble. Fry the bacon until crisp and drain on paper towels. Wipe the skillet clean of the excess fat and cook the eggs until set. Turn off the heat and add the cottage cheese and shredded cheddar cheese and mix well. Cool and serve. Refrigerate any leftovers for up to three days.

🐾 Put a whole package of bacon in a glass casserole dish and spread the slices out. Bake in the oven at 375 degrees for about 30 minutes, depending on your oven. There is no need to turn the bacon as it cooks through. Be sure to put foil loosely on the top so you don't get bacon splatters all over your oven. Freeze for later use.

🐾🐾 You can use any shredded cheese you have on hand.

🐾🐾🐾 Sour cream may also be substituted for the cottage cheese.

ZUCCHINI YUM -YUM

1 (6 ounce) can cat food, any flavor

1/4 cup zucchini, unpeeled, uncooked, and shredded

1/4 cup instant brown rice, cooked

2 tablespoons cottage cheese, small curd

Break up the cat food in a small bowl. Add the shredded zucchini, brown rice, and the cottage cheese. Mix well and serve. Refrigerate any leftovers for up to three days.

🐾 Shred a whole zucchini in a food processor and refrigerate for later use. Green or yellow zucchini may be used, whichever one is on sale. The green zucchini are firmer and easier to shred.

🐾🐾 Cook up several cups of the instant brown rice to have on hand in the refrigerator for the week.

THANKSGIVING AGAIN

1 cup turkey, cooked and shredded

1/4 cup leftover white or sweet potatoes, mashed

1/4 cup lettuce, shredded

3 tablespoons low-fat chicken broth

Shred the turkey into a small bowl. Add the mashed potatoes, either the white or the sweet, along with the shredded lettuce. Mix well and add the broth as needed. Refrigerate any leftovers for up to three days.

🐾 Dark turkey meat is easier to shred.

🐾🐾 If using the leftover sweet potatoes, rinse off any marshmallows or brown sugar that may be on them and then mash.

🐾🐾🐾 Use carrots, green beans, or other leftover vegetable you have on hand in place of the lettuce, although cats do like the shredded lettuce.

CRUNCHY ROAST BEEF

2 cups roast beef, cooked

1/4 cup dry cat food

2 tablespoons carrots, cooked or raw

2 tablespoons beef broth

Place the roast beef, dry cat food, carrots, and beef broth in a food processor. Process until blended well. Add more broth if needed. Refrigerate any leftovers for up to three days.

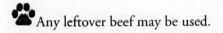Any leftover beef may be used.

Substitute any vegetable your cat likes.

LIVER & RICE

1 cup chicken livers, cooked

2 tablespoons instant brown rice, cooked

2 tablespoons zucchini, shredded, uncooked, and unpeeled

1 teaspoon catnip

Cook the chicken livers in a skillet with a little olive oil for about 15 minutes over medium heat. Drain and let cool and then cut into bite size pieces. Place in a bowl and add the cooked rice. Place the zucchini in a food processor and pulse until shredded, or grate on a box grater. Add this to the liver and rice mixture and mix well. Refrigerate any leftovers for up to three days.

🐾 Beef liver can be substituted for the chicken livers.

🐾🐾 Add a sprinkle of garlic powder to the liver as it is cooking.

PARSLEY SALMON

1 can (6 ounce) salmon, drained

1 hard boiled egg, chopped

2 tablespoons parsley, chopped

2 tablespoons cottage cheese, small curd

Place the salmon in a bowl and break up. Add the chopped egg, parsley, and cottage cheese. Mix well and serve. Refrigerate any leftovers for up to three days.

BREAKFAST MEOW

1 can (6 ounce) cat food, any flavor

1 slice bacon, cooked and crumbled

1 large egg, whisked

2 tablespoons cheddar cheese, grated

1 tablespoon catnip

Cook the bacon in a skillet and drain on paper towels. Wipe the skillet clean and add the egg and cook until done. Turn off the heat and add the cat food, cheddar cheese, and catnip. Mix well and let cool. Refrigerate any leftovers for up to three days.

🐾 Use any grated cheese you have on hand

In Conclusion

These wonderful creatures that God created were given to us to love and to protect. Their dependence is solely on their master, so it is up to us to make them as healthy and happy as we can. In return for our small effort, we get the unconditional love and dedication that only dogs can give and ask nothing in return.

I urge you to cook just one or two meals a week, or ideally for the whole week, and see your dog healthier and happier and living longer than the expected.

Thank you for purchasing this book and a portion of the proceeds will be donated to the National Canine Cancer Foundation.

REFERENCES

www.fda.gov
www.petdiets.com
www.pets.com
www.thedogscene.com
www.aspca
www.usda.gov
www.aafco
www.wearethecure.org